J. B. Priestley

When We Are Married

A Yorkshire Farcical Comedy

with an Introduction by
E. R. WOOD

HEINEMANN EDUCATIONAL BOOKS LTD
LONDON

Heinemann Educational Books Ltd

LONDON MELBOURNE EDINBURGH
TORONTO JOHANNESBURG
SINGAPORE AUCKLAND IBADAN
HONG KONG NEW DELHI
NAIROBI

ISBN 0 435 22712 2

First published 1938
Copyright John Boynton Priestley 1938
First published in Hereford Plays Series 1971

Published by
Heinemann Educational Books Ltd
48 Charles Street, London W1X 8AH
Printed in Great Britain by
Cox & Wyman Ltd
London, Fakenham and Reading

Contents

INTRODUCTION

John Boynton Priestley was born in Bradford in 1894, the son of a schoolmaster. On leaving school he went to work in the local wool trade, and at the age of sixteen he was already writing pieces for Bradford newspapers. He served in the army throughout the war of 1914–1918, and on demobilization in 1919 he was awarded a government grant which enabled him to go to Trinity Hall, Cambridge. At the university he supplemented his grant by writing, and after taking his degree he settled in London to make literature his profession.

He achieved a series of reputations in different spheres. At first he was a literary critic and essayist; among his early books were *The English Comic Characters*, *The English Novel*, and scholarly biographies of Peacock and Meredith. Next he began to write novels, and in 1929 everybody was reading and praising *The Good Companions*, which made him famous all over the world. Over the next thirty years this was followed by a score of successful novels. Then in 1932 he began a new career – as a dramatist. *Dangerous Corner* was the first of some twenty-five plays covering a wide range, from popular comedy such as *When We Are Married* to ambitiously experimental dramas like *Johnson Over Jordan* and *Music at Night*. In the thirties J. B. Priestley was deeply involved at the very heart of the theatre world; he became a theatre director, closely associated with the most prominent actors and directors; he even took over once, at twenty-four hours' notice, the leading part of Ormonroyd in *When We Are Married*. At this time he was determined to give the public something more than the conventional 'West End success'; to make them feel or think more deeply and more originally; and at the same time to hold his own financially in the theatre industry. He had some disappointments, but on the whole his plays were very popular.

During the last war he established a new reputation, this time as a broadcaster; by his *Postscripts* to the Sunday night news bulletins he did much to sustain people's spirit with his forthright common sense and humanity, and the BBC's Overseas service made his personality well-known over the world. After the war he was chosen as a delegate to UNESCO.

He has written film scripts and television plays, books about his travels and books about people, as well as many articles on public affairs. There are three volumes of autobiography: *Rain upon Godshill* (1937); *Midnight on the Desert* (1939) and *Margin Released* (1962). Among his critical works are *The Art of the Dramatist, Literature and Western Man* and *The Edwardians*, which recall the academic bent of his early years. In 1964 he published a large work on a theme that has long fascinated him, *Man and Time*.

His powerful personality adds vigour to everything he writes; he is never dull. In the preface to *Delight*, a collection of short essays on the things in life that he enjoys, he says that he is often considered to be 'too blunt, brusque and downright difficult', but he protests, 'Actually I am amiable and rather shy.' His essays and more personal writings give the impression of zest for life as it is, combined with a reformer's ideas of what it might be and a philosopher's awareness of its mystery.

For the student of J. B. Priestley the most useful books of literary criticism are *J. B. Priestley, An Informal Study of his Work* by David Hughes (Hart Davis 1958), *J. B. Priestley the Dramatist* by Gareth Lloyd Evans (Heinemann 1964) and *J. B. Priestley: Portrait of an Author* by Susan Cooper (Heinemann 1970).

When We Are Married was first presented on the London stage in 1938. It has enjoyed a robust life ever since in provincial repertories and in dramatic societies, but when it was revived in 1970 in a major West End production, some critics seemed surprised that 'The Priestley magic still worked'. An article in *The Times* described as 'a mystery' the current success in the London theatre of 'old brands for regular customers'. The assumption had evidently been that nothing could be expected to interest and amuse the modern playgoer unless it expressed the preoccupations of the moment in the tone and style of today. If this were really so, we should have to scrap everything from Shakespeare to Shaw. Fortunately, however, audiences and readers can still laugh at basically comic situations and the eternal folly of human beings, even in an age when 'traditional' is often assumed to be a word of disparagement or even scorn.

It is true, of course, that there have been marked changes, within the last decade or two, in the taste of audiences – in what they expect to laugh at in theatre or cinema, or in front of the television screen. The pace has quickened. Audiences respond with laughter or applause to sly allusions, which do not need to be very witty so long as they are up-to-date. They have been trained to do this by the prompting of studio audiences on radio and TV, or even by pre-recorded laughter and applause. This may be one reason why Molière and Sheridan in the theatre now seem a little slow, over-explicit, even laboured, by modern standards, and Shakespeare is not considered funny enough unless pepped up and made to sound like our contemporary.

A deeper change in the spirit of comedy may be seen in the attitude to the institutions and values of the community. Classical comedy is the product of a stable society. By holding up to ridicule the follies and failings of men and women it bolsters up the standards of common sense and the virtues of moderation and reasonable conformity; the conventional happy ending fortifies the belief that all is well when reason prevails.

But ours is an age of shifting values and collapsing conventions, in which laughter tends to be more destructive, iconoclastic, subversive; any revered aspect of society may become fair game for mockery; even sanity itself may be the butt of goonish laughter, and logic is challenged by the comedy of the absurd. The happy ending now seems a naïve contrivance out of key with the spirit of the age, in which the line between comedy and tragedy is blurred.

The analysis attempted above is not to be taken too literally; it depends on generalizations and over-simplifications which would be modified in a full discussion of the subject. For example, it must be admitted that comedy has always made fun of foibles peculiar to the age presented; Elizabethan young men affecting the fashionable melancholy of the time, or Restoration fops ludicrously involved in duelling, have their counterparts today; but the differences are more apparent than the essential resemblances. Again, bitter and subversive comedy is not a new phenomenon, nor has the distinction between tragedy and comedy always in the past been as precise as theorists would like. And of course the new elements have left large areas of the entertainment world unchanged. Comedians are still exploiting nightly the old situations and time-mellowed jokes for the delight of large audiences of ordinary people. Even 'Old Time Music Hall' has a strong nostalgic appeal; and while the audience masquerades as Granny's generation it becomes obvious that in the theatre we can laugh and marvel at much the same things as in the old days. So it should surprise nobody that there is a large and appreciative audience for plays like *When We Are Married*.

If you think that *When We Are Married* is a period piece you are right. It was so intended when J. B. Priestley wrote it, for he set it thirty years back, in 1908. In 1938 he was recalling the Yorkshire folk he had known in his boyhood. The characters should not be played as grotesques; they are not, as a recent critic suggested, 'figures from an old Blackpool postcard'. The author has made this quite clear. 'The plot is nonsensical,' he has written, 'but the characters and their attitudes and their talk are all authentic.' This is what West Riding people were really like, and they are not different in essentials today.

Of course, some features of the scene are changed since 1908; more than young people of today may realize. The idea that respectable couples may have been living together for twenty-five years without being legally married would create less sensation nowadays than in 1908 or even 1938. This change does not 'date' the play in a sense that matters, for the supposed loophole in the marriage laws was never more than a device for a wry reassessment of married life by its victims or beneficiaries; but it does reduce the shock of the revelation as a source of mirth in the theatre.

The young may be more incredulous of the reactions of the middle-aged in the play to 'carrying-on'. In the affair of Gerald and Nancy there is not a suspicion of anything that would invite the mildest disapproval of older people today. The heavy censure of the 'big men at chapel' was never justifiable, but such puritan severity was once confused with virtue and duty. Our grandparents in an audience might have found it hypocritical and tyrannical, but not at all incredible.

Another social change in our time is the virtual disappearance of domestic service as a part of middle-class home life, and as a focus of useful discord in plays. Our grandmothers talked of little else but the shortcomings of the servants if they had any, and if they belonged to the servant class they were much preoccupied by the faults of their mistresses. The replacement of domestics by the impersonal washing machine and the taciturn automatic cooker has robbed the theatre of rich material for comedy. Mistresses like Maria Helliwell were perhaps not so unfailing a source of comedy in themselves as a cause of comedy in their servants, such as the rebellious and forthright Mrs Northrop and the perky Ruby Birtle.

Ruby belongs to an old tradition of the cheeky young servant who has more sense than the people she waits on. This is not to say that she is a stock type: on the contrary, she has plenty of personality of her own, which comes alive in the flavour of her local speech and blunt manner. Her attitude to romance and marriage is drily sceptical; she is so free of sentiment that she talks (Ormonroyd tells her) as if she had been brought up in a tram-shed – a tram-shed in the West Riding of Yorkshire.

In several other characters of the play we can see this quality of belonging to a particular period and local way of life, and at the same time to the general comic tradition. Among the eternal human foibles that have always been matter for comedy – and always will be – are snobbery, pomposity and self-satisfaction (here presented with a spicing of West Riding chapel hypocrisy). They are qualities which grow and stiffen with age. So does intolerance of young people. Classical comedy tends to see the world from the point of view of the young and to present the old and the middle-aged in an unfavourable light. This is understandable. As we get stiffer in our joints we become more rigid in our opinions and attitudes – and one lesson taught by comedy is the value of flexibility. The actor playing Albert Parker in the 1970–71 production of *When We Are Married* walked, sat and stood stiffly, so that his physical appearance reflected his mental and emotional rigidity. Parker behaves and talks like an automaton: his response to a situation is so predictable that others can anticipate and chorus his words. Nothing dents the armour of his complacency; he is so unaware of what his wife must think of him that he can actually say to her, 'I've sometimes thought that right at first you didn't realize just what you'd picked out o' t'lucky bag.' One of the benefits of comedy is that it allows us to examine specimens like Albert Parker, who would be insufferable in real life, and to see them deflated amidst laughter, without the sting of malice which would be ugly in an actual showdown. Moreover, a comedy can end in more general goodwill than would be probable in real life, so that Councillor Parker, having seen himself as others see him, makes an effort to do better henceforth. His last words in the play offer some hope: 'I say we'll have some fun'; then he joins in the singing.

Joe Helliwell is pompous, hypocritical, self-satisfied, but more human than Albert Parker. There is no suggestion that he is stingy, like Parker. Advancing age has not dried him up, but rounded and reddened him. He enjoys some of the good things of life. He appreciates 'a fine lass and a good sport' when he meets one in Blackpool. He can be expansive and genial, and we could perhaps wink at his 'bit of fun' with Lottie if he were not so self-righteous about the 'carrying-on' of others.

Councillor Parker and Alderman Helliwell have a feature in common which easily provokes the ridicule of less exalted citizens – their overweening pride in their public position, what Whitman called 'the never-ending audacity of elected persons.' In a democracy we accept the service of such men to the community, but ungratefully question their motives, among which self-importance seems prominent. No doubt they in their turn suspect that our laughter (if they are aware of it) is tinged with jealousy. Anyhow, elected persons have been the butt of jokes since Caligula made his horse a Consul.

We are not all doomed to be Councillor Parkers or Alderman Helliwells: in the play the middle-aged have deteriorated in varying degrees. Herbert Soppitt, being perhaps too modest, has merely declined into a hen-pecked husband – a favourite joke in the theatre, and always capable of arousing laughing sympathy when the worm turns (as in *When We Are Married*) and the mild victim becomes the stern and inexorable victor.

What about Ormonroyd? Like Falstaff, he is a drunken reprobate. Why is he more likeable than his respectable contemporaries? Perhaps because he can laugh at himself. Like Falstaff, he has a zest for Life. ('Ormonroyd: "Lets 'ave a bit o' life, I say." Falstaff: "Give me life, say I".') Like him, he extols the virtues of drink. Intoxication loosens the tongue and relaxes inhibitions, and so suits the comic purposes of the playwright. He can impose control at will, so that it does not become tedious or disgusting, as sometimes happens in reality. Thus drunkenness as presented on the stage can be consistently funny, and more congenial than prim sobriety, to which it offers a robust challenge.

A common human weakness which is made fun of in *When We Are Married* is provincialism, and here the West Riding atmosphere is relevant and genuine:

> As soon as they told me he's a southerner and his name's Gerald I said 'We don't want him' I said. 'La-di-dah, that's what you're going to get from him', I said.

This may seem corny to sophisticated London critics, but to a Yorkshireman it has the ring of truth. In the West Riding village where I was brought up we *knew* as a fact that the farther down south you travelled the more affected, effeminate and effete you would find the natives to be. (If this is less obvious today, my schoolfellows would say, it is because so many Yorkshiremen have moved south to show the southerners how to work and live.) On the basis of such geographical and sociological theory, Northerners would unite in applauding Ormonroyd's view of Torquay (which is as far 'down South' as you can get):

> a favourite all year round resort of many delicate and refined persons of genteel society. In other words, it's a damned miserable hole.

We can all share his scorn for a wife who would choose to leave the bracing air of the West Riding for the life-in-death of a genteel resort on the South Coast of Devonshire.

But local patriotism seen from within may look like ignorant provincialism from without. And if you narrow its scope it becomes more vulnerable to the mockery of ampler spirits. Civic pride in Clecklewyke (a combination of the real Heckmondwyke and Cleckheaton) looks like petty parochialism even from provincial Leeds or Bradford. In *When We Are Married* the scope is still further narrowed to the sphere of local chapels. We may sympathize with the view that 'what we want is a bit o' good old Yorkshire organ-playing', but when it is only to boost the triumph of Lane End Chapel over Hillroad Baptists, Tong Congregational and Picklebrook Wesleyans, we may begin to see the ridiculous jealousies of this tiny world as Gulliver saw those of the Lilliputians.

The main theme of the play is, of course, marriage. The title recalls with a touch of irony the once-popular duet:

> When we are married . . .
> – Why, what will you do?
> – I'll be as sweet as I can be to you;
> I will be tender
>   – And I will be true
> When I am married, sweetheart, to you.

What happens to such tender sentiments after twenty-five years of holy wedlock is no laughing matter . . . at any rate to those involved. Why, then, is it so funny on the stage? We are tickled by the incongruity of the harsh realities when set against the sentimental assumptions. When the dreamily eloquent Ormonroyd, improvising on the theme of the marriage vows, talks of married life as 'a bee-yutiful thing – side by side – hand in hand – through all life's sunshine and storms – always with a loving smile – in sickness and health – rich or poor', his tipsy emotion is punctured by the practical Ruby: 'When I've tried going side by side and 'and in 'and for twenty minutes I've 'ad more than I want.' Anyhow, we know that Ormonroyd didn't travel far with his loving smile through life's sunshine and storms before his wife left him for a boarding house in Torquay. And we hear the brides of twenty-five years ago exclaiming their real feelings: 'I've been married to you for twenty-five years and it's time I had a rest' and 'if you'd had twenty-five years of *him* . . .', all the more amusing because this is the occasion of a conventional celebration.

These outbursts on marriage are incongruous – but true. Most wives feel like this at times, even if they don't say what they feel. For how insufferable even the best of husbands can be, with their condescension to women, their assumption that they always take charge, their embarrassing taste for making speeches when the women want to chat, their wearying efforts to be witty, their dreary anecdotes about what Sir Harold said, their drearier talk about business and the fall in the price of Merinos, and their sneaking off together to the Club! But then, how maddening all wives can be, with their 'Oh, Albert, must you?', their fussing about who thought of it first, their giving you the best years of their lives, and even their dark threats, 'You'll hear more of this when I get home'; for when it comes to bullying, how much worse a woman can be than a mere man! The most powerful personality on the distaff side, Clara Soppitt, reminds us of Wilde's assessment: 'Twenty years of romance makes a woman look like a ruin, but twenty years of marriage makes her something like a public building.' She is the one among the wives, like Albert Parker among the husbands, who most deserves to be cut down to size, and the final taming of this shrew, signified by her submissive 'Yes, Herbert', provides one of the strands in the happy ending.

You may be sceptical about a happy ending which depends on a change of character so fixed by long habit as Albert Parker and Clara Soppitt, and perhaps we ought not to take it too seriously. The others have taken stock of the sunshine and the storms; they have had a glimpse of freedom and decided that they prefer their bondage. Married life may not be all that is promised in the song, but for many people it can be surprisingly happy and comfortable from time to time. The play does not seek to probe deep into the hostilities in which marriages break up.

The happy ending is a feature of comedy that is out of fashion in our gloomier or more realistic times. In the old days everybody expected a tidying up of loose ends and a general reconciliation before the curtain fell. A comedy such as *When We Are Married* is a mixture of reality and artifice. The reality is in the characters and their environment, the artifice is in the shaping of the plot, for real life rarely has tidy shape. The material of this play is craftsman-built to ensure that it is most effective when acted before an audience. Notice how situations are comically reversed, and patterns repeated with variations. When the three chapel elders are browbeating Gerald, Albert Parker is the most brutal, Joe Helliwell a bit inclined (in view of the festive occasion) to give youth a second chance, and Herbert Soppitt mildly conciliatory; but when Gerald snatches the upper hand with his bombshell from the Rev. Beech, they change their tune, so that Parker and Helliwell become ingratiating and even turn on the innocent Soppitt for having been too hasty. The shock of Gerald's discovery that Beech was not qualified to solemnize marriages is inflicted with dramatic and comic effect on the husbands, then repeated on the wives, with still more explosive reactions. We are then all agog to see and hear the confrontation of husbands and wives.

The reversal of roles in the Soppitt household is essentially a stage situation. Herbert's rebellion is most enjoyable when seen as well as heard. It smoulders sulkily until Clara slaps him, then blazes out noisily, spreads to wither the astounded Parker, and continues to give warm satisfaction to the end. It is visually funnier if Herbert is physically small and Clara four-square, but the main source of laughter is the change in Herbert when he realizes that if he isn't married to Clara, he need not submit to her dictatorship. Herbert ought to have married Annie, who makes a parallel stand against her tyrant-husband, and it is amusing to speculate how Albert might have got on if he had married Clara.

The organization of everything is directed to stage effect; some of the funniest moments in the play are visual rather than verbal. For instance, there is a moment when Ormonroyd, having closed his eyes while Ruby was reciting, opens them to find a totally different figure – the massive Clara – staring at him from where Ruby stood. His bewilderment hardly needs words to set the audience laughing. Ruby's recitation is an entertainment added as an extra gift to actress and audience, having no necessary place in the plot. It makes us laugh because of the incongruity between Ruby's flat unemotional voice and the sentimentality of Mrs Hemans's verses. A similar stage turn which enriches the show without influencing the action is the duet sung by Lottie and Ormonroyd, 'just for old times' sake'. This is an appropriate occasion to sing 'When We Are Married'. It has the sort of tune which can make the whole world kin, for while some can smile at the sentimentality which others enjoy, all can come away from the theatre humming it. The play itself has some of the same universal quality, providing unpretentious, easy entertainment for all.

CAST OF FIRST LONDON PERFORMANCE

Produced at the St Martin's Theatre, London, on *11* October *1938* with the following cast:

RUBY BIRTLE	Patricia Hayes
GERALD FORBES	Richard Warner
NANCY HOLMES	Betty Fleetwood
HELLIWELL	Lloyd Pearson
MRS HELLIWELL	Muriel George
PARKER	Raymond Huntley
MRS PARKER	Helena Pickard
SOPPITT	Ernest Butcher
MRS SOPPITT	Ethel Coleridge
MRS NORTHROP	Beatrice Varley
FRED DYSON	Alexander Grandison
HENRY ORMONROYD	Frank Pettingell
LOTTIE GRADY	Mai Bacon
REV CLEMENT MERCER	Norman Wooland

Produced by Basil Dean

CAST OF 1970 PRODUCTION

The 1970 *When We Are Married* opened at the Strand Theatre, London, on 11 November. The play was presented by Paul Elliott and Duncan C. Weldon, with the Yvonne Arnaud Theatre, in association with Peter Bridge.
The cast was as follows:

RUBY BIRTLE	Shirley Steedman
GERALD FORBES	Jonathan Lynn
MRS NORTHROP	Gretchen Franklin
NANCY HOLMES	Jennifer Agnew
FRED DYSON	James Rowe
HENRY ORMONROYD	Fred Emney
ALDERMAN JOSEPH HELLIWELL	William Moore
MARIA HELLIWELL	Freda Jackson
COUNCILLOR ALBERT PARKER	Frank Thornton
HERBERT SOPPITT	Hugh Lloyd
CLARA SOPPITT	Peggy Mount
ANNIE PARKER	Gwen Cherrell
LOTTIE GRADY	Daphne Anderson
REV. CLEMENT MERCER	Brian Hewitt-Jones

The play was directed by Robert Chetwyn and designed by Gerald Kitching.

WHEN WE ARE MARRIED

A Yorkshire Farcical Comedy

CHARACTERS

RUBY BIRTLE

GERALD FORBES

NANCY HOLMES

ALDERMAN JOSEPH HELLIWELL

MARIA HELLIWELL

COUNCILLOR ALBERT PARKER

ANNIE PARKER

HERBERT SOPPITT

CLARA SOPPITT

MRS NORTHROP

FRED DYSON

HENRY ORMONROYD

LOTTIE GRADY

REV. CLEMENT MERCER

The sitting-room of Alderman Helliwell's house in Cleckleywyke, a town in the West Riding, on a September evening about thirty years ago.

ACT ONE

The sitting-room in HELLIWELL'S *house, a solid detached late-Victorian house. On left (actor's left) wall is a window. Left of centre in back wall is a door to rest of house, leading directly into the hall. On right wall is a small conservatory, with door leading into this, and then into garden. The room is furnished without taste in the style of about thirty years ago. There is an upright piano. Little cupboards, drawers, small tables, etc. At rise, evening sunlight coming through window. Nobody on stage.*

We hear the front door bell ring. A moment later, RUBY BIRTLE *ushers in* GERALD FORBES. RUBY *is a very young 'slavey' of the period, who looks as if her hair has just gone 'up'.* FORBES *is a pleasant young man, in the smart clothes of the period, and unlike* RUBY *and most of the other characters does not talk with a marked West Riding accent.*

RUBY: You'll have to wait 'cos they haven't finished their tea.

GERALD: Bit late, aren't they?

RUBY (*approaching, confidentially*): It's a do.

GERALD: It's what?

RUBY: A do. Y'know, they've company.

GERALD: Oh – I see. It's a sort of party, and they're having high tea.

RUBY (*going closer still*): Roast pork, stand pie, salmon and salad, trifle, two kinds o' jellies, lemon cheese tarts, jam tarts, swiss tarts, sponge cake, walnut cake, chocolate roll, and a pound cake kept from last Christmas.

GERALD (*with irony*): Is that all?

RUBY (*seriously*): No, there's white bread, brown bread, currant teacake, one o' them big curd tarts from Gregory's, and a lot o' cheese.

GERALD: It *is* a do, isn't it?

RUBY (*after nodding, then very confidentially*): *And* a little brown jug.

GERALD (*astonished*): A little brown jug?

RUBY (*still confidentially*): You know what that is, don't you? *Don't* you? (*Laughs.*) Well, I never did! Little brown jug's a drop o' rum for your tea. They're getting right lively on it. (*Coolly.*) But you don't come from round here, do you?

GERALD (*not disposed for a chat*): No.

   A distant bell rings, not front door.

RUBY: I come from near Rotherham. Me father works in t' pit, and so does our Frank and our Wilfred.

   Distant bell sounds again.

GERALD: There's a bell ringing somewhere.

RUBY (*coolly*): I know. It's for me. Let her wait. She's run me off me legs today. And Mrs Northrop's in t' kitchen – she can do a bit for a change. There's seven of 'em at it in t' dining-room – Alderman Helliwell and missus, of course – then Councillor Albert Parker and Mrs Parker, and Mr Herbert Soppitt and Mrs Soppitt – and of course, Miss Holmes.

GERALD: Oh – Miss Holmes *is* there, is she?

RUBY: Yes, but she's stopped eating. (*Giggles. Coolly.*) You're courting her, aren't you?

GERALD (*astonished and alarmed*): What!

RUBY (*coolly*): Oh – I saw you both – the other night, near Cleckley Woods. I was out meself with our milkman's lad.

   GERALD *turns away.*

Now don't look like that; I won't tell on you.

GERALD (*producing a shilling, then rather desperately*): Now – look here! What's your name?

RUBY: Ruby Birtle.

GERALD: Well, Ruby, you wouldn't like Miss Holmes to get into a row here with her uncle and aunt, would you?

RUBY: No, I wouldn't like that. But I'd like that shilling.

GERALD (*after giving it to her*): You said Miss Holmes had finished eating.

RUBY: Yes. She can't put it away like some of 'em. I'd rather keep Councillor Albert Parker a week than a fortnight. D'you want to see her?

GERALD: Yes. Could you just give her the tip quietly that I'm here – if the rest of them aren't coming in here yet?

RUBY: Not them! You'd think they'd been pined for a month – way they're going at it! I'll tell her. She'd better come round that way – through t' greenhouse—

Before she can actually move, MRS NORTHROP, *an aggressive but humorous working-woman of about fifty puts her head in the door.*

MRS NORTHROP (*aggressively*): Oh – 'ere y'are!

RUBY (*coolly*): That's right, Mrs Northrop.

MRS NORTHROP (*aggressively*): I see nought right about it – you gassin' in 'ere as if you owned t' place instead o' gettin' on wi' your work. She's rung for yer twice, an' I've just taken another lot o' hot water in. Nah, come on, yer little crackpot!

Holds door open, and RUBY *goes to it – turns and grins. Exit* RUBY.

MRS NORTHROP: Aren't you t' organist at chapel?

GERALD: Yes.

MRS NORTHROP (*cheerfully*): Ay, well, they've got it in for you.

GERALD (*astonished*): How do you know?

MRS NORTHROP: 'Cos I 'eard 'em say so. (*Complacently.*) I don't miss much.

GERALD: So that's why Mr Helliwell asked me to come round and see him.

MRS NORTHROP: That's right. There's three of 'em 'ere tonight, d'you see – all big men at chapel. You've been enjoyin' yerself a bit too much, I fancy, lad.

GERALD: So that's it – is it?

MRS NORTHROP (*with very confidential air*): Ay – and d'you know what I say? I say – to 'ell with 'em!

Goes out, leaving GERALD *looking a little worried. He moves about restlessly, takes cigarette-case out of his pocket mechanically, then puts it back again. He keeps an eye on the door into conservatory. After a few moments,* NANCY HOLMES, *an attractive girl in her early twenties, hurries in through this door.*

NANCY (*in breathless whisper*): Gerald!

GERALD: Nancy! (*Makes as if to kiss her.*)

NANCY (*breathlessly*): No, you mustn't, not here – no, Gerald – please—

But he does kiss her and no harm has been done.

Now, listen, Gerald, and be sensible. This is serious. You know why Uncle Joe sent for you?

GERALD (*with a light grin*): They've *got it in for me.* I've just been told.

NANCY: It's serious, Gerald. They've been grumbling about you some time, and now, as far as I can gather, one of these miserable old beasts saw you late one night – with *me*—

GERALD (*serious now*): Oh – I say – you weren't recognized, were you?

NANCY: No. But *you* were.

GERALD: Well, that's not so bad, as long as they can't drag you into it. I know how strict your aunt is, and you can't afford to quarrel with them here until we're ready to be married—

NANCY (*earnestly*): No, but you can't either, Gerald. And they're going to be very cross with you, and you'll have to be awfully careful what you say to them. And there's that beastly Councillor Parker here too, and you loathe him, don't you?

GERALD: Absolutely. And I'll loathe him more than ever now that he's full of roast pork and trifle. I think I'd better give them time to recover from that huge ghastly tuck-in they're having.

NANCY: I should. Though they've nearly finished now.

GERALD: If I clear out for half an hour or so, could you slip away too?

NANCY: I might. They don't really want me. I'm in the way.

You see, it's an anniversary celebration, and I don't come into it at all.

GERALD: What are they celebrating?

Before she can reply, RUBY *opens door, announcing:*

RUBY: It's *Yorkshire Argus* – two of 'em.

GERALD *rises, moves down right.* NANCY *rises up to door. Enter* FRED DYSON, *a cheerful, rather cheeky youngish reporter, and* HENRY ORMONROYD, *who carries a large and old-fashioned newspaperman's camera and a flash-light apparatus. Ormonroyd is a middle-aged man with an air of beery dignity and wears a large drooping moustache.* DYSON *walks down to* NANCY.

RUBY: This is Miss Holmes, Alderman Helliwell's niece. T'others is still having their tea.

RUBY *goes out.*

DYSON (*cheerfully*): 'Evening, Miss Holmes. (*To Gerald.*) How d'you do? This is Mr Henry Ormonroyd, our photographer.

ORMONROYD (*bowing*): Pleased to meet you, I'm sure. Delightful weather we're having for the time of year.

GERALD: Isn't it?

ORMONROYD (*profoundly*): It is.

DYSON: We seem to have come too early.

NANCY: I'm afraid you have—

ORMONROYD (*with dignified reproach*): What did I tell you, Fred? Always wanting to rush things. We could have had at least a couple more – with my friend at the Lion. He's a chap who used to have a very good little peppermint-rock business on the Central Pier, Blackpool, at the time I had my studio – there. Old times, y'know, Mr – er, and happy days, happy days! (*Hums.*)

DYSON (*briskly*): All right, Henry. I'm sorry we're early. Matter of fact, I don't know yet what this is about. I just got a message from the office to come up here and bring a photographer.

NANCY: You see, it's their Silver Wedding.

DYSON: Henry, it's Alderman Helliwell's *Silver Wedding*.

ORMONROYD: Very nice, I suppose.

NANCY: Yes, but not only my uncle and aunt's. There were three couples – my uncle and aunt, Mr and Mrs Soppitt, Mr and Mrs Parker—

DYSON: Is that Councillor Albert Parker?

NANCY (*pulling a little face*): Yes. You know him?

DYSON (*gloomily*): Yes, we know him.

ORMONROYD: Every time he opens his mouth at the Town Hall, he puts his foot in it, so they call him 'the foot and mouth disease'. Ha Ha. Are all three happy couples here?

NANCY: Yes, because they were all married on the same morning at the same chapel. They have a photograph – a combined wedding group. (*She goes to find it – top of piano.*)

GERALD: You'll have to interview 'em, and they'll tell you how happy they've been—

DYSON: Oh – yes. I see the idea now.

NANCY (*returning with old photograph*): Here you are. All six of them on their wedding morning. Don't they look absurd in those clothes?

ORMONROYD (*solemnly*): To you – yes. To me – no. I was married myself about that time. (*Holding photograph at arm's length.*) Now, you see, Fred, what's wanted is another group in the very same positions. After twenty-five years' wear and tear. Very nice.

DYSON: You're holding it upside down.

ORMONROYD: I know, lad. I know, that's the way we always look at 'em professionally. Either flies 'ave been at this or somebody's touched up Albert Parker with a screw-driver. Well, if we're too early, we're too early. Might nip back to the Lion, Fred lad, eh?

ORMONROYD *takes camera from top of settee left.*

DYSON: We'll come back in about an hour.

ORMONROYD: They're keeping a very nice drop of beer down at the Lion now.

DYSON *and* ORMONROYD *go out,* NANCY *going towards the door with them, and shutting it behind them.* GERALD *looks at*

*the photograph, then at the back of it, and is obviously interested
and amused.*

GERALD: This was when they were all married then –
September the fifth, Eighty-Three?

NANCY: Yes – why? What's the matter, Gerald? (*He has
started laughing.*) Gerald, what is it? Oh – don't be so mean.
They'll be here in a minute.

*As he shakes his head, still laughing softly, we hear voices
behind door into hall.*

GERALD: They're coming in. Nancy, let's dodge out that way.

*Puts photograph on table behind settee right, picks up his straw
hat, while she has gone to door into conservatory, and they hurry
out that way, shutting door behind them.*

*Voices outside door into hall are louder now, and after a
moment the* PARKERS, *the* SOPPITTS, *the* HELLIWELLS *enter.
They are dressed in their best, and obviously crammed with high
tea.* ALBERT PARKER, *is a tall, thin, conceited, sententious man,
his wife* ANNIE, *a hopeful kind of woman.* HERBERT SOPPITT
is a smallish neat man, clearly dominated by his wife CLARA, *a
noisy woman. The* HELLIWELLS *are high-coloured, rather
bouncing, rather pompous, very pleased with themselves. Their
ages are all between forty-five and fifty-five.* HERBERT SOPPITT
and MRS PARKER *talk a rather genteel ordinary English; the
other four have pronounced north-country accents, with particularly
broad 'a' sounds.*

HELLIWELL (*very much the host*): Now what's wanted now's a
good cigar, an' I've got the very thing. (*Goes to get box from
drawer or table.*)

MARIA (*indignantly*): That Mrs Northrop! When she's finished
her washing-up tonight she goes – and goes for good.

CLARA: And quite right too! They're all the same. Answering
back – if you say anything.

MARIA: Trouble with her is – she likes a drop. I've smelt it
before today.

CLARA *sits below sofa left.* MARIA *to corner.* ANNIE *drops
down right to sofa down right.*

HELLIWELL (*offering cigar-box to Parker*): Now then, Albert! You'll find that's a good cigar, La Corona.

PARKER (*taking one*): Thanks Joe. As you know, I don't smoke a lot, but when I do, I like a good cigar.

HELLIWELL (*offering to Soppitt*): Herbert?

SOPPITT: I don't think – er – I will – thanks, Joe.

MARIA (*expansively*): Nay, Herbert, 'ave one o' Joe's cigars.

CLARA: If he'd had it to pay for himself, he'd have been wanting one.

SOPPITT (*rather nervously*): I think – I'd rather not smoke just now – I believe I ate too much at tea.

ANNIE (*to keep him company*): I know *I* did.

PARKER (*severely*): Yes, an' you'll be complaining before the night's out.

CLARA: An' so will Herbert.

PARKER (*complacently*): Now that's something that never bothers me.

HELLIWELL: No, we've noticed that, Albert.

PARKER (*offended*): How d'you mean?

MARIA: Go on, Albert, you know what Joe is – must 'ave his little joke.

ANNIE: I know *I* ought to have stopped long before I did – I mean, at tea – but, Maria, everything was *so* nice.

CLARA: 'Ere, 'ere.

MARIA (*complacently accepting this*): Well, I said to Joe 'Now, Joe,' I said, 'we'll only have the six of us, but we'll make it an occasion an' do it well while we're at it,' I said. Didn't I, Joe?

HELLIWELL (*busy attending to his cigar, though he does not remove the band*): Did you?

MARIA (*indignantly*): You know very well I did.

HELLIWELL (*still not interested*): All right, you did then.

MARIA (*same indignant tone*): You know quite well I did, Joe Helliwell.

HELLIWELL (*suddenly annoyed himself*): All right, all right, all right, you did then.

CLARA (*pats Maria's hand*): They're all alike. Wait till somebody else's with you, and then try to make you out a liar.

PARKER (*severely*): Speak for yourself! I don't try to make my
wife out a liar, do I, Annie?

ANNIE (*rather timidly, hesitantly*): Well – no – Albert, not –
really—

PARKER (*very severely*): How d'you mean – *not really* – I just
don't, that's all. (*Changing the subject, in rather lordly style.*) A
good smoke, Joe, quite a good smoke. It reminds me of that
cigar Sir Harold Watson gave me not so long since at the
club. I was standing near the fireplace, and Sir Harold came
up—

ANNIE (*gathering courage to interrupt*): Albert – you told them
before.

PARKER (*glaring*): Well, I can tell 'em again, can't I?

SOPPITT: Maria, have you got a copy of that old photograph
we had taken? I couldn't find ours.

MARIA: Yes. Where is it, Joe? (*While he looks round.*) Aaa, I
laugh many a time when I think o' that morning – six of us,
all so nervous—

HELLIWELL: And the parson worse still. He was only like
two-pennorth o' copper, an' I could ha' given him a few
years myself.

CLARA: I think we were about first he'd ever married.

ANNIE: I'm sure we were. I didn't feel I'd been married
properly—

PARKER (*severely*): Of course you'd been married properly.
If he'd been ninety and doing it all his life, you wouldn't ha'
been married any better, would you?

MARIA: I've forgotten his name now. He was only a tempo-
rary, wasn't he?

SOPPITT: I remember! (*A pause.*) It was a tree. Beech.

HELLIWELL: That's right – Beech – an' he'd a funny squint.
(*Has found photograph.*) And here's the old photo.

    Hands it to his wife and the ladies look at it, with exclamations,
while the men remain aloof.

PARKER (*the business man now*): I see Crossbreds are down again.

HELLIWELL (*another business man*): Ay – and they'll stay down with Australian market as it is. If I've said it once, I've said it a thousand times – if Merinos is down and staying down, then your Crossbreds'll have to follow. Now, look at Merinos—

MARIA (*looking up to expostulate*): Here, Joe, we didn't come here to talk about Merinos. This isn't Wool Exchange. Take a look at yourselves and see what we took on.

He ignores her. She puts photograph on table back of settee.

HELLIWELL: Now wait a minute. 'Ealths!

MARIA: That's right, Joe. Ring!

HELLIWELL *rings.* MARIA *turns to others.*

We ought to do it in proper style, an' drink our healths before we go any further.

SOPPITT (*attempting a joke*): Further – where?

CLARA (*severely*): That'll do, Herbert. A bit o' fun's all right, but you go too far.

SOPPITT: I didn't mean—

CLARA (*cutting in*): That'll do.

MRS NORTHROP *looks in.*

MRS NORTHROP (*aggressively*): Well?

MARIA (*rather grandly*): There's a tray with glasses on – just bring it in—

MRS NORTHROP (*indignantly*): What – me? How many pairs of 'ands—

HELLIWELL (*peremptorily*): *Now then* – just tell thingummytite – Ruby – to bring in the port wine.

MRS NORTHROP: What – on top o' your tea? You'll be poorly.

She withdraws. HELLIWELL *is furious.*

HELLIWELL (*angrily*): Now did you 'ear that—

MARIA (*hastily*): All right, Joe, we don't want any trouble. She goes tonight, an' she doesn't come back.

CLARA: I don't know what things are coming to! All the same! Answering back!

PARKER (*sententiously*): They're all alike, that class of people. We have the same trouble at mill. Don't know when they're well off. Idle, that's what they are – bone idle!

CLARA: *And* impudent! Back-answers!

ANNIE (*timidly*): Yes – but I suppose they don't know any better—

PARKER (*severely*): They know a lot better. And what you want to stick up for 'em for, I can't think.

HELLIWELL (*heartily*): Now then, Albert, don't start fratching, but try an' enjoy yourself for once. This is an anniversary. Which reminds me, Charlie Pearson told me, t' other day, they built a new Wesleyan Methodist Chapel up at Thornton, and they opened with an anniversary. Anyhow, this is ours, so let's have peace an' goodwill all round. Now I thought we'd first drink a bit of a toast to ourselves—

MARIA: That was *my* idea.

HELLIWELL (*ignoring this, but only just*): Then I thought we'd have a bit of a chat about old times, an' then we'd settle down to a game o' Newmarket—

MARIA: That was my idea too.

HELLIWELL (*annoyed*): What the hangment does it matter whose idea it was, so long as we get on with it and enjoy ourselves!

SOPPITT: That's the great thing. (*Controlled belch. Catches his wife's eye and falters.*) Enjoy ourselves. (*Rises. Moves to door. Looks miserable and a bit sick.*)

CLARA (*severely*): I told you to leave that salmon alone.

HELLIWELL: Nay, Clara, why can't he have a bit o' salmon if he fancies it?

CLARA (*sharply*): 'Cos it doesn't fancy him, Joe Helliwell, that's why. Look at that time we all went to Scarborough!

SOPPITT (*turns*): It was Bridlington.

CLARA: It was both! And what did that doctor say? *You're digging your grave with your teeth, Mr Soppitt.*

a

HELLIWELL: Hahaha!

Enter RUBY, *carrying tray with six small glasses on it, and three bottles of port.*

Here, what did you want to bring 'em all for? One bottle at a time's enough.

RUBY (*putting down tray*): Mrs Northrop said you'd better 'ave t'lot while you was at it.

HELLIWELL: In future, just take your orders from me and not from Mrs Northrop. Now just trot along – an' no lip. (*Starts to take cork out of bottle.*)

RUBY (*turning at door*): Mrs Northrop says she's not coming 'ere again—

HELLIWELL (*heatedly*): We know all about it. (*Moves after her, cigar in mouth, bottle in hand.*)

MARIA (*cutting in*): Now let it be, Joe.

HELLIWELL *stands, draws cork with an effort.*

RUBY *has now gone and closed door.* HELLIWELL *begins pouring out the port.*

D'you know what we ought to do for this? We ought to get just in the same places we were in that old photo. Where is it? (*Finds it and directs them from it.*) Now here we are. (*Uses a sofa.*) I was in the middle. You were here, Clara. You this side, Annie. Now come on, Albert – behind Annie. Herbert.

MARIA *sits last. These five have now arranged themselves in grouping of old photograph.* HELLIWELL *hands them their glasses of port, then takes up a position himself.*

HELLIWELL (*facetiously*): Here's to me and my wife's husband!

MARIA: Let's have none o' that silly business, Joe!

PARKER (*solemnly*): A few serious words is what's needed.

ANNIE (*rather plaintively*): Oh – must you, Albert?

PARKER: How d'you mean – must I? What's wrong with a few serious words on an occasion like this? Marriage – is a serious business.

CLARA: That's right, Albert. Where'd we be without it?

SOPPITT: Single.

CLARA: That'll do, Herbert.

PARKER (*sententiously*): Marriage – well – marriage – to begin
with, it's an institution, isn't it?

MARIA (*solemnly*): That is so. (*Sighs profoundly.*)

PARKER (*getting into his stride*): One of the *oldest* institutions. It
goes back – right back to – well, it goes right back. And it's
still going strong today. Why?

HELLIWELL (*hastily*): Well, because—

PARKER (*sharply cutting in*): Let me finish, Joe, let me finish.
Now why is it still going strong today? Because it's the
backbone of a decent respectable life.

HELLIWELL (*solemnly*): True, Albert, true.

PARKER: Where would women be without marriage?

CLARA (*sharply*): And where'd some o' you men be?

PARKER: All right, I'm coming to that.

HELLIWELL: Well, don't be too long, Albert. I want to try
this port.

PARKER (*solemnly*): Marriage may be a bit more necessary to
women than it is to men—

ANNIE: Why?

PARKER (*annoyed at this*): *Why?*

HELLIWELL: Children, you see, Annie.

ANNIE (*abashed*): Oh – yes – I'd forgotten. Still—

PARKER: I'm talking now, *if* you please. But if a woman wants
a 'ome and security and a respectable life, *which* she gets
from marriage, a man wants something to—

CLARA (*quickly*): He wants all he can get.

PARKER: He wants a nice comfortable 'ome, somebody to tell
his troubles to and so forth—

HELLIWELL (*facetiously*): That's good, Albert, the *and so forth*.

PARKER: Now, Joe—

HELLIWELL: Well, cut it short—

PARKER (*slowly and solemnly*): So, as we're all gathered 'ere to
celebrate the anniversary of our joint wedding day, friends,
I give you – the toast of *Marriage*!

MARIA: Very nice, Albert.

They all drink.

ANNIE (*confidentially*): It'll go straight to my head. D'you remember that time at Harrogate? I could have sunk through the floor when that waiter laughed.

HELLIWELL (*producing bottle again*): Now wait a minute. That's all right as far as it goes – but – nay – damn it!—

MARIA (*reproachfully*): Joe!

HELLIWELL: We must have another toast, just for ourselves. I bet it isn't often there's three couples can meet like this who were all wed on same morning together. Now then—

Insists on filling the glasses again as they still hold them in their hands.

MARIA (*confidentially*): I don't act silly, but my face gets so red.

HELLIWELL: Now – here's to all of us – and the Reverend Mr What's his name – Beech – who tied us up – wherever he is—

THE OTHERS: Here's to us. Here's to him. (*Etc.*)

They drink. When they have finished, front-door bell is heard.

MARIA: Front door! Who'll that be?

HELLIWELL (*rather importantly*): Well, I told *Yorkshire Argus* to send somebody round to have a word with us.

CLARA (*delighted*): What – are you going to have a piece in the papers?

PARKER: They don't want to catch us like this.

PARKER *swallows rest of his port hastily. The others do the same. The group breaks up.*

RUBY *looks in.*

MARIA: Is it *Yorkshire Argus*?

RUBY: No, it's Mr Forbes, t'organist from t'chapel. He came afore, an' then went away again.

HELLIWELL: Tell him to wait.

RUBY *goes.* HELLIWELL *turns to the others.*

You know about this business, Albert. You too, Herbert.

SOPPITT (*hesitantly*): Yes – but— (*Crosses to Helliwell.*)

HELLIWELL (*sharply*): But, nothing. You're too soft, Herbert.

CLARA: I'm always telling him so.

HELLIWELL: He's chapel organist – he's paid for t'job – an' either he behaves himself properly or he goes.

PARKER (*severely*): He'll go anyhow, if I've *my* say.

ANNIE: No, Albert, he's not a bad young fellow—

PARKER: Now you shut up, Annie. You don't know half of what we know. An' I'll bet we don't know half there is to know about that chap. Never should ha' been appointed. I said so then. I say so now. I know my own mind.

ANNIE (*rebelliously*): I wish sometimes you'd keep a bit of it to yourself.

PARKER: What's that mean?

NANCY *now appears at door from conservatory.*

MARIA: Hallo, love, where've you been?

NANCY (*who seems a trifle giggly*): Just out a minute. You don't want me, do you, Auntie? Because if you don't, I thought I'd put my hat and coat on and see if Muriel Spencer's in. (*Crosses up to door.*)

MARIA (*rises*): All right. There's that Gerald Forbes waiting outside – your uncle has something to say to him – now don't go talking to him.

HELLIWELL: I should think not. Just say 'Hello' or 'Good evening' and leave it at that. The less you have to do with that chap the better, Nancy.

NANCY *suddenly explodes into giggles.*

Now what's funny about that?

NANCY (*still giggling*): I'm sorry, Uncle. I just remembered – something that amused me—

NANCY *goes out, giggling.*

HELLIWELL: Now what's got hold of her?

MARIA: Oh – she's at silly age. They don't know half the time whether to laugh or cry when they're that age. Now, Clara – Annie – we'll leave the men to it. I expect that's what they want—

PARKER (*solemnly*): Certainly. After all, it's chapel business.

MARIA: Well, we want to go upstairs anyhow!

HELLIWELL: That's right.

CLARA *glares at him.*

MARIA: You haven't seen what Joe bought me yet. But don't take too long over him.

PARKER: *Him!* It wouldn't take *me* long—

HELLIWELL: It'll take me less long, 'cos I don't make speeches. Here, we'll put these out o' t'way— (*at sideboard.*)
    The women go out, and HELLIWELL *puts the glasses back on the tray. A certain primness now descends on them.*

PARKER: I said from first – it's a bad appointment. To start with, he's too young.

SOPPITT (*rather timidly*): I don't think that matters much.

PARKER (*severely*): Trouble with you, Herbert, is you don't think anything matters much, and that's just where you're wrong.

HELLIWELL: Young Forbes is a southerner an' all.

PARKER (*with grim triumph*): Ah – I was coming to that.

SOPPITT: Oughtn't we to have him in?

HELLIWELL: No, let him wait a bit.

PARKER: Do him good. No, as soon as they told me he's a southerner and his name's Gerald, I said: 'We don't want him.' I said 'La-di-dah. That's what you're going to get from him,' I said. 'Lah-di-dah. What we want at Lane End – biggest chapel for miles – wi' any amount o' money in congregation – what we want is a bit o' good old Yorkshire organ-playing and choir training,' I said. 'We don't want la-di-dah.' (*With awful imitation of ultra-refined accents.*) 'Heow d'yew dew. Sow chawmed to meek your acquaintance. Eoh, de-lateful wethah!' Grr. You know what I call that stuff?

SOPPITT (*who has a sense of humour*): Yes. (*Broadly.*) La-di-dah.

HELLIWELL: Albert's right. We made a mistake. Mind you, he'd good qualifications, an' he seemed a nice quiet lad. But I must say, after old Sam Fawcett, chapel didn't seem right with an organist who goes round wearing one o' these pink shirts and knitted ties and creases in his trousers—

PARKER: It's all—

Here SOPPITT *joins in.*

PARKER *and* SOPPITT: La-di-dah!

PARKER (*in disgusted tone*): Then look at his *Messiah*! We
warned him. I said to him myself: 'I know it's a Christmas
piece, but you've got to get in quick, afore the others.'

HELLIWELL: Right, Albert. After t'end o' November, there's
been so many of 'em you might as well take your *Messiah*
an' throw it into t'canal.

PARKER: And look what happened. Hillroad Baptist gave
Messiah. Salem gave *Messiah*. Tong Congregational gave
Messiah. Picklebrook Wesleyans gave *Messiah*. And where
was Lane End?

SOPPITT: Well, when we did get it – it was a good one.

HELLIWELL: I'm not saying it wasn't, but by that time who
cared? But anyhow all that's a detail. Point is, we can't have
any carrying on, can we?

SOPPITT (*gravely*): Ah – there I agree, Joe.

PARKER (*indignantly*): An' I should think so. Organist at Lane
End Chapel *carrying on*! That sort o' game may do down
south, but it won't do up 'ere.

HELLIWELL: We're all agreed on that.

    SOPPITT *and* PARKER *nod.*

Right then! We'll have 'im in.

    HELLIWELL *goes to the door, the other two sitting up stiffly
    and looking official and important.*

(*Rather grimly through open door.*) All right, come in.

    GERALD FORBES *follows him in, closing but not latching the
    door behind him.* GERALD *looks cool and self-possessed, with a
    twinkle in his eye.* HELLIWELL *sits down and looks as official
    and important as the other two. All three stare severely at Gerald,
    as he sits down.* GERALD *pulls out a cigarette-case, but no sooner
    has he taken a cigarette from it than* ALBERT PARKER *remon-
    strates with him.*

PARKER (*severely*): I wouldn't do that.

GERALD (*rather startled*): Do what?

PARKER (*severely*): Well, what 'ave you got in your 'and?

GERALD (*still surprised*): This? Cigarette. Why?

PARKER: Under the circumstances, young man, don't you think it might be better – more – more suitable – more fitting – if you didn't smoke that just now?

>   *The three men look at each other.*

GERALD (*with a shrug*): Oh – all right, if that's how you feel about it. (*Puts case away. A pause.*) Well? You wanted to talk about something, didn't you?

HELLIWELL (*firmly*): We did. We do.

PARKER: And if I'd 'ad *my* way, we'd have been talking to you long since.

GERALD: Well, not very long since, because I haven't been up here very long.

PARKER: No, you haven't been up here very long, and I don't think you'll be up here much longer.

HELLIWELL: Here, Albert, let *me* get a word in. Mr Forbes, you're organist of our Lane End Chapel, and that's the biggest place o' worship round here, and this is a very respectable neighbourhood, with a lot o' money behind it. You have a paid appointment as organist and choir-master.

GERALD: Yes, though it doesn't keep me, y'know, Mr Helliwell.

HELLIWELL: No, but because you *are* our organist, you're able to get pupils and various extra jobs, so you don't do so bad out of it, eh?

GERALD (*a trifle dubiously*): No, I'm quite satisfied – for the time being.

PARKER (*annoyed*): *You're* satisfied! For the time being! You're satisfied!

GERALD (*quietly*): That's what I said, Mr Parker.

PARKER (*with dignity*): Councillor Parker. (*Pointing.*) Alderman Helliwell. Councillor Parker. *Mr* Soppitt.

GERALD (*indicating himself*): Plain mud!

PARKER (*explosively*): Now listen—

HELLIWELL (*cutting in noisily*): Nay, let me finish, Albert. We want to keep calm about this – just keep calm.

GERALD: I'm quite calm.

HELLIWELL (*explosively*): You're a damn sight too calm for my liking, young man. You ought to be sitting there looking right ashamed of yourself, instead of looking – looking – well, as you do look.

GERALD: But you haven't told me what's wrong yet.

PARKER (*angrily*): Wrong? You're wrong. And carrying on's wrong.

HELLIWELL (*loftily*): In some chapels they mightn't care what you did – I don't know – but Lane End's got a position to keep up. We're respectable folk, and naturally we expect our organist to behave respectably.

SOPPITT (*apologetically*): I think you have been very careless, Mr Forbes, and there really has been a lot of grumbling.

PARKER: For one thing – you've been seen out – late at night – wi' girls.

GERALD: Girls?

HELLIWELL: It may be t'same lass each time, for all I know, but if what I hear is true, whoever she is, she ought to be ashamed of herself. My word, if she'd owt to do wi' me, I'd teach her a sharp lesson.

PARKER: Somebody saw you once gallivanting away late at night, at Morecambe. And it gets round, y'know – oh – yes – it gets round.

GERALD (*beginning to lose his temper*): Yes, so it seems. But I didn't think you'd find it worth while to listen to a lot of silly gossip—

PARKER (*sharply*): Now don't start taking that tone—

GERALD: What tone can I take? I say, a lot of silly gossip—

SOPPITT: Now, steady, steady.

GERALD: Silly gossip. Old women's twaddle—

HELLIWELL (*heavily*): That'll do. Just remember, you're not much more than a lad yet. We're nearly twice your age, and we know what's what—

GERALD (*angrily*): Well, what is what then?

HELLIWELL (*angrily*): This is what. We're not going to have any more of this. Either behave yourself or get back to where you came from. You're not going to make us a laughing-stock and a byword in t'neighbourhood. Now this is a fair warning—

GERALD (*steadily*): I haven't done anything I'm ashamed of.

PARKER: What's that prove? If a chap's got cheek of a brass monkey, he never need do aught he's ashamed of.

SOPPITT: Careful, Albert.

PARKER: Why should I be careful? I'll tell him to his face what I've said behind his back. He never ought to have been appointed, and now he's been carrying on and not caring tuppence what respectable folk might think, he oughtn't to be given any warnings but told to get back to where he came from, and then he can carry on as much as he likes.

   Both GERALD *and* HERBERT SOPPITT *start to protest, but* HELLIWELL *loudly stops them.*

HELLIWELL: Now, Albert, we mustn't be too hard. We must give young men just another chance. (*Severely and patronizingly to Gerald.*) I'm not sure I should if this were any other time. But nay – damn it, this is a festive occasion an' we must take it easy a bit. So I'm giving you a last chance to mend yourself. And you can think yourself lucky catching me i' this humour. Just happens we're all celebrating anniversary of our wedding day – all three of us – ay, we've all been married twenty-five years today. (*Blows nose.*)

   GERALD *shakes his head rather sadly.*

What're you shaking your head about?

GERALD (*quietly, gently*): Well, you see, Mr Helliwell – I beg your pardon, Alderman Helliwell – I'm rather afraid you haven't been married twenty-five years.

HELLIWELL (*roaring*): Do you think we can't count, lad?

GERALD (*same quiet tone*): No, I don't mean that. But I'm afraid you've only been living together all this time.

HELLIWELL (*jumping up angrily*): *Living together!* I'll knock your head right off your shoulders, lad, if you start talking like that to me.

GERALD (*also standing up*): No, no, no. I'm not trying to insult you. I mean what I say.

PARKER (*rises, angrily*): Mean what you say! You're wrong in your damned 'ead.

OPPITT (*authoritatively, for him*): Wait a minute – Albert, Joe. We must listen. He means it.

HELLIWELL (*angrily*): Means it! Means what?

GERALD (*impressively*): If you'll just be quiet a minute I'll explain.

PARKER (*explosively*): I don't want to—

GERALD (*sharply*): I said – *quiet*.

HELLIWELL: Leave him be, Albert.

GERALD (*sits*): Thanks. Mind if I smoke now?

All sit. With maddening slowness, GERALD *takes out and lights cigarette.* HELLIWELL *and* ALBERT PARKER *watch him with impatience and look as if about to explode.*

I went to North Wales for my holiday this summer—

HELLIWELL (*impatiently*): Is this part of it, 'cos *I* don't care *where* you went for your holidays!

GERALD (*calmly*): I went to North Wales, and only came back about a fortnight ago. While I was there I made the acquaintance of a parson, who'd been in Africa for the last twenty years. When he learnt that I was the organist of Lane End Chapel, Cleckleywyke, he became very excited, and then it turned out that he'd been at Lane End himself for a short time. About twenty-five years ago.

OPPITT: What was his name?

GERALD: Beech. Francis Edwin Beech.

HELLIWELL (*boisterously*): Oh – yes – Beech! We were only talking about him tonight. We remember Mr Beech. He married us, y'know. Yes, he married us, five-and-twenty years ago – all three couples. That's what we're celebrating—

His voice suddenly dies away because he realizes what the other two have realized for the last minute, that there might be something wrong. So as he mutters the end of his sentence now, he glances unhappily at the others.

Y'know – being – married – twenty-five years—
    GERALD *looks at them over his cigarette.*

PARKER (*swallowing*): Go on. Go on.

GERALD: I could see that something he rememberd about
    Cleckleywyke and Lane End worried him. (*With obvious
    relish.*) You might say, gentlemen, it was *preying* on hi
    mind, it was *gnawing* at his conscience, it was *haunting* him
    it was—

HELLIWELL (*angrily*): What is this – a recitation?

GERALD: I must apologize if I'm boring you, gentlemen—

PARKER (*in sudden passion, jumps up*): La-di-dah! La-di-dah
    (*As* GERALD *stares at him in astonishment.*) Now if you've
    anything to tell us, for God's sake tell us – and don'
    la-di-dah!

HELLIWELL: Quite right, Albert. (*To Gerald, impatiently.*
    Well, what did Mr Beech say?

GERALD: He didn't *say* anything.

    HELLIWELL *and* PARKER *are at once relieved and annoyed
    They breathe more freely, but then feel they have been needlessl
    alarmed.* HERBERT SOPPITT *waits to learn more and look
    steadily at Gerald.*

HELLIWELL: Well, what are you nattering on about hin
    for—?

SOPPITT: Just a minute, Joe. (*To Gerald.*) That's not all, is it

GERALD: All? I should think not! Only you won't give me a
    chance. I said he didn't *say* anything, but he *wrote* something
    The letter only came two days ago. I have it here. (*Produce
    one rather small sheet of notepaper, written on both sides. He nov
    reads it impressively.*) From the Reverend Francis Edwir
    Beech. '*Dear Mr Forbes, Before returning to Africa I feel I ow
    it both to you and to myself to explain what you must have foun
    puzzling in my many references to Cleckleywyke and Lane En
    Chapel. Although I was only temporarily at Lane End, I coul
    not forget it; for there I was guilty of the most culpable negligence.*
    The three men look at each other.
'*I went to Cleckleywyke straight from college, and during thos*

first few months I did not realize that there were various forms I ought to have signed, and had witnessed by church officers, so that one may be recorded as an authorized person to perform the ceremony of marriage—'

HELLIWELL (*rises, shouting*): What? (*Grabs the letter from Gerald, stares at it, then reads himself, slowly.*) . . . *'the ceremony of marriage. The result was, I was not then an authorized person. Fortunately during that short period I was only called upon twice to marry people, but the first time there were no less than three hopeful young couples who imagined – poor souls – that I was joining them in holy wedlock – when – I – was completely – unauthorised – to – do – so—'*

PARKER (*yelling and snatching the letter*): Let's have a look. (*He looks and* HERBERT SOPPITT *joins him.*) It's signed all right too – Francis Edwin Beech.

GERALD: And if you compare that signature with the one in the chapel register, you'll see it's the same man. No deception.

HELLIWELL (*dazed and bitter*): Why – the bloody donkey!

HELLIWELL, PARKER *and* SOPPITT *look at each other in silent consternation.*

SOPPITT (*slowly, thoughtfully*): Why, if we've never been married at all, then—

HELLIWELL: Don't start working it out in detail, Herbert, 'cos it gets very ugly – very ugly. There's that lad o' yours at grammar school for instance – I wouldn't like to have to give him a name now—

SOPPITT (*indignantly*): Here, steady, Joe—

HELLIWELL: Well, you see, it gets very ugly. Keep your mind off t'details.

PARKER (*bitterly*): Silver wedding!

HELLIWELL: Now don't you start neither, Albert.

PARKER (*solemnly*): Joe, Herbert, when them three poor women upstairs gets to know what they really are—

HELLIWELL (*grimly*): Then t'balloon goes up properly. Talk about a rumpus. You'll 'ear 'em from 'ere to Leeds.

PARKER (*gravely*): Joe, Herbert, they mustn't know. Nobody
must know. Why – we'd be laughed right out o' town.
What – Alderman Helliwell – Councillor Albert Parker –
Herbert Soppitt – all big men at chapel too! I tell you, if
this leaks out – we're done!

HELLIWELL: We are, Albert.

SOPPITT (*horrified*): If once it got into the papers!

HELLIWELL (*even more horrified*): *Papers!* Oh – Christmas! –
it's got to be kept from t'papers.

    GERALD *who has been leaving them to themselves to digest this
news, now turns to them again.*

GERALD (*holding out his hand*): You'd better give me that letter,
hadn't you?

PARKER and HELLIWELL (*rising*): Oh no!
    They stand together as if protecting it.

PARKER (*holding it out*): This letter—

HELLIWELL (*snatching it*): Here—

PARKER (*angrily*): Nay, Joe – give it back—

HELLIWELL: I'm sorry, Albert, but I don't trust nobody wi
this letter but meself. Why – it's – it's dynamite!

GERALD: Yes, but it's addressed to me, and so it happens to be
my property, you know.

SOPPITT: I'm afraid he's right there!

HELLIWELL (*turning on him, annoyed*): You would have to put
that in, wouldn't you? Dang me, you're in this mess just as
we are, aren't you?

PARKER (*severely*): Anyhow, *we've* a position to keep up even
if you haven't, Herbert.

SOPPITT (*apologetically*): I was only saying he's right when he
says it's his property. We had a case—

HELLIWELL (*aggressively*): Never mind about that case. Think
about this case. It's a whole truck-load o' cases, this is.

GERALD: My letter, please.

HELLIWELL (*ingratiatingly*): Now listen, lad. I know you only
want to do what's right. And we happened to be a bit
'asty with you, when you first came in. We didn't mean it

Just – a way o' talking. When Herbert Soppitt there gets started—

SOPPITT (*indignantly*): What – me!

PARKER (*severely*): You were 'asty, y'know, Herbert, you can't deny it. (*To Gerald.*) Mind you, I'll say now to your face what I've often said behind your back. You gave us best *Messiah* and best *Elijah* we've ever had at Lane End.

HELLIWELL: Easy, easy! Best i' Cleckleywyke! And why! I've told 'em when they've asked me. 'That young feller of ours is clever,' I said. 'I knew he had it in him,' I said.

SOPPITT (*hopefully*): Yes, you did, Joe. (*To Gerald.*) And so did I. I've always been on your side.

GERALD: I believe you have, Mr Soppitt. (*To all three of them.*) You can keep that letter tonight – on one condition. That Mr Soppitt has it.

SOPPITT (*eagerly, holding out his hand*): Thank you, Joe.

HELLIWELL (*uneasily*): What's the idea o' this?

GERALD: That happens to be the way I feel about it. Now either give it back to me at once – or hand it over to Mr Soppitt, who'll be answerable to me for it.

SOPPITT (*eagerly*): Certainly, certainly.

HELLIWELL *silently and grudgingly hands it over.* SOPPITT *puts it carefully in his inside pocket. The others watch him like hawks. There is a pause, then we hear a knocking from upstairs.*

HELLIWELL: Knocking.

PARKER (*grimly*): I 'eard.

HELLIWELL: That means she's getting impatient.

PARKER: I expect Clara's been ready to come down for some time.

HELLIWELL (*bitterly*): They want to get on with the celebration.

PARKER (*bitterly*): Chat about old times.

HELLIWELL (*bitterly*): Nice game o' cards.

GERALD (*after a pause*): I'd better be going.

HELLIWELL (*hastily*): No, no. No. Take it easy.

PARKER: No 'urry, no 'urry at all. I expect Joe has a nice cigar for you somewhere.

HELLIWELL (*with forced joviality*): Certainly I have. And a drink of anything you fancy—

GERALD: No, thanks. And I must be going.

HELLIWELL: Now listen, lad. We've admitted we were 'asty with you, so just forget about it, will you? Now you see the mess we're in, through no fault of ours— (*Goes up to get cigars.*)

GERALD: I do. And it *is* a mess, isn't it? Especially when you begin to think—

PARKER (*hastily*): Yes, quite so, but don't you bother thinking. Just— (*rather desperately*) try an' forget you ever saw that letter.

HELLIWELL (*who now comes with the cigars*): We're all friends, the best of friends. Now you've got to have a cigar or two, lad – I insist— (*he sticks several cigars into Gerald's outside pocket, as he talks*) and you're going to promise us – on your word of honour – not to tell anybody anything about this nasty business, aren't you?

All three look at him anxiously. He keeps them waiting a moment or two.

GERALD: All right.

They breathe again. HELLIWELL *shakes his hand.*

HELLIWELL: And you won't regret it, lad.

The knocking from upstairs is heard again.

PARKER (*miserably*): 'Ear that?

HELLIWELL: It's wife again.

SOPPITT (*thoughtfully*): Curious thing about wives. They're always telling you what poor company you are for them, yet they're always wanting to get back to you.

HELLIWELL (*darkly*): That isn't 'cos they enjoy your company. It's so they can see what you're doing.

PARKER: Well, what are we doing?

HELLIWELL (*sharply now*): Wasting time. (*To them.*) Now

listen, chaps, we're in no proper shape yet to face t'wives. They'd have it all out of us in ten minutes, and then fat'll be in t'fire.

PARKER: I know. We've got to put our thinking caps on.

SOPPITT: I suppose Mr Beech couldn't have been mistaken, could he?

PARKER: We might take that letter and get expert advice—

HELLIWELL (*hastily*): What! An' 'ave it all over the town?

PARKER (*quickly*): We might put a case – without mentioning names—

HELLIWELL (*with decision*): I know what we'll do. We'll nip down to t'club, 'cos we can talk it over there in peace an' quiet. Come on, chaps. Just as we are, straight down t'club. (*To Gerald.*) Now, young man, you promised. You won't go back on your word?

GERALD: No. You're safe with me.

HELLIWELL (*urgently*): Good lad! Now, wait till we've got off, then go out front way. Come on, Albert, Herbert, we've no time to lose an' we go this way— (*bustling them towards exit through conservatory*) straight to t'club.

They go out. GERALD *looks at his watch, smiles, lights a cigarette, then makes for door, which has never been quite closed. When he opens it suddenly,* MRS NORTHROP, *still holding a towel and a large glass dish, which she is wiping perfunctorily, is discovered just behind door. She is in high glee and not at all abashed at being found there.*

GERALD (*with mock sternness*): Have you been listening?

MRS NORTHROP (*who may have had a drink or two*): Listening! I should think I have been listening! I wouldn't have missed this lot even if it means 'aving earache for a week. None of 'em rightly married at all! Not one of 'em properly tied up! (*She begins laughing quite suddenly, and then goes off into peals of laughter, rolling against the door. The dish she holds seems to be in danger.*)

GERALD (*amused as he goes past her, out*): Look out – or you may break that dish.

D

MRS NORTHROP (*calling to him*): Brek a dish! If I want to, I'll brek a dozen now.

GERALD (*just off, challengingly*): Not you! I dare you!

MRS NORTHROP (*coolly*): Well, here's a start, any road. (*Tosses the dish down and it smashes noisily in hall.*)

We hear GERALD *give a laughing shout, then bang the front door.*

MRS NORTHROP *now starts laughing helplessly again, still leaning against the door.*

MRS NORTHROP: Nay – dammit!— (*laughing*) Oh dear – oh dear – oh dear—

She is still roaring with laughter as the curtain briskly descends.

END OF ACT ONE

ACT TWO

About half an hour later. The lights are on. MARIA *is drawing curtains,* ANNIE *and* CLARA *are laying out the cards and counters for Newmarket on a card-table, and they continue doing this throughout the scene that follows, chiefly counting the coloured counters and putting them into piles.*

CLARA (*with much discontent*): Well I must say – this is a queer way o' going on.

MARIA: They'll have just gone outside to finish their smokes.

CLARA (*grimly*): When Herbert takes me out to enjoy myself, I don't expect him to be outside finishing any smokes.

ANNIE (*at table*): Perhaps they'd something they wanted to talk over.

CLARA: Well they can talk it over here, can't they?

    RUBY *enters from conservatory.*

MARIA: Well, Ruby, are they out there?

RUBY: No, they aren't.

MARIA (*sharply*): Have you looked properly?

RUBY: Well I couldn't miss three grown men in a garden that size.

MARIA: Did you look up and down the road like I told you?

RUBY: Yes, but they aren't there.

    The three wives look at each other, puzzled.

CLARA: Didn't you hear them go?

RUBY: No. I was back in t'kitchen all time, doing t'washing-up. That Mrs Northrop left me to it.

MARIA: Where was she then?

RUBY: Out 'ere somewhere, I fancy. I know she's gone like a dafthead, ever since she come back. Laughin' to herself – like a proper barmpot.

MARIA: Well, ask Mrs Northrop if she knows where they went.

    RUBY *goes.*

That noise you heard upstairs was a bit o' this Mrs Northrop's work – one o' my best dishes gone. An' Ruby says she just laughed.

CLARA: Stop it out of her wages and see if she can get a good laugh out o' that. I've no patience with 'em.

ANNIE: I thought she didn't look a nice woman.

CLARA: One o' them idle drinking pieces o' nothing from back o' t'mill.

MARIA: Well, I was in a hurry and had to have somebody. But she goes – for good – tonight.

    RUBY *appears.*

RUBY: Mrs Northrop says they wanted to have a nice quiet talk, so they went down to their club.

    RUBY *disappears.*

CLARA (*angrily*): Club! *Club!*

ANNIE: And tonight of all nights – I do think it's a shame.

MARIA (*indignantly*): I never 'eard o' such a thing in me life.

CLARA (*furiously*): *Club!* I'll club him.

ANNIE: Nay, I don't know what's come over 'em.

CLARA (*angrily*): I know what'll come over one of 'em.

MARIA: Perhaps there's something up.

CLARA: Something down, you mean – ale, stout, an' whisky. Drinks all round! Money no object!

MARIA: They're 'ere.

    The three of them immediately sit bolt upright and look very frosty. The men file in from the conservatory, looking very sheepish.

HELLIWELL (*nervously*): Ay – well—

MARIA (*grimly*): Well what?

HELLIWELL: Well – nowt – really.

SOPPITT (*nervously*): We didn't – er – think you'd be down yet. Did we, Joe? Did we, Albert?

HELLIWELL: No, we didn't, Herbert.

ALBERT: That's right, we didn't.

CLARA (*cuttingly*): Herbert Soppitt, you must be wrong in your head. *Club!*

ANNIE: And tonight of all nights!

HELLIWELL: Well, you see, we thought we'd just nip down for a few minutes while you were talking upstairs.

MARIA: What for?

PARKER: Oh – just to talk over one or two things.

CLARA: What things?

SOPPITT: Oh – just – things, y'know – things in general.

PARKER (*coming forward, rubbing his hands*): Well – I see the table's all ready – so what about that nice little game o' Newmarket?

CLARA: You'll get no Newmarket out o' me tonight.

ANNIE: You're – you're – selfish.

CLARA: Have you just found that out? Never think about anything but their own comfort and convenience.

MARIA: I'm surprised at you, Joe Helliwell – and after I'd planned to make everything so nice.

CLARA: Lot o' thanks you get from them! Club! (*Looking hard at* SOPPITT.) Well, go on – say something.

The men look at each other uneasily. Then the women look indignantly.

ANNIE: Just think what day it is!

CLARA: And after giving you best years of our life – without a word o' thanks.

MARIA: An' just remember, Joe Helliwell, there were plenty of other fellows I could have had besides you.

ANNIE: You seem to think – once you've married us you can take us for granted.

PARKER (*uneasily*): Nay, I don't.

CLARA (*very sharply*): Yes, you do – all alike!

MARIA: If some of you woke up tomorrow to find you weren't married to us, you'd be in for a few big surprises.

HELLIWELL (*uneasily*): Yes – I dare say – you're right.

MARIA (*staring at him*): Joe Helliwell, what's matter with you tonight?

HELLIWELL (*uneasily*): Nowt – nowt's wrong wi' me, love.

CLARA (*looking hard at Soppitt*): You'll hear more about this when I get you 'ome.

SOPPITT (*mildly*): Yes, Clara.

The women look at the men again, then at each other. Now they turn away from the men, ignoring them.

MARIA: What were you saying about your cousin, Clara?

CLARA (*ignoring the men*): Oh – well, the doctor said: 'You're all acid, Mrs Foster, that's your trouble. You're making acid as fast as you can go.'

ANNIE: Oh – poor thing!

CLARA: Yes, but it didn't surprise me, way she'd eat. I once saw her eat nine oyster patties, finishing 'em up after their Ethel got married. I said: 'Nay Edith, have a bit o' mercy on your inside,' but of course she just laughed.

The men have been cautiously moving to the back towards the door. As HELLIWELL *has his hand on the handle,* MARIA *turns on him.*

MARIA: And where're you going now?

HELLIWELL (*uneasily*): Into t'dining-room.

MARIA: What for?

HELLIWELL: Well – because – well— (*Gathers boldness.*) We've summat to talk over. Albert, 'Erbert, quick!

They file out smartly, without looking behind them. The women stare at them in amazement. The door shuts. The women look at each other.

MARIA: Now what's come over 'em?

ANNIE: There's something up.

CLARA: What can be up? They're just acting stupid, that's all. But wait till I get his lordship 'ome.

ANNIE: Suppose we went home now—

CLARA: No fear! That's just what they'd like. Back to t'club!

MARIA: I'd go up to bed now and lock me door, if I didn't think I'd be missing something.

ANNIE: It's a pity we can't go off just by ourselves – for a day or two.

CLARA: And what sort o' game are they going to get up to while we're gone? But I've a good mind to go in and tell mine: 'Look, I've been married to you for five-and-twenty years and it's about time I had a rest.'

MARIA: And for two pins I'll say to Joe: 'If you got down on your bended knees and begged me to, I wouldn't stay married to you if I didn't have to.'

Door opens slowly, and MRS NORTHROP *comes just inside, carrying large string bag, with clothes, two stout bottles in, etc. She is dressed to go home.*

MRS NORTHROP: I've done.

MARIA (*suspiciously*): It hasn't taken you very long.

MRS NORTHROP (*modestly*): No – but then I'm a rare worker. Many a one's said to me: 'Mrs Northrop, I can't believe you've just that pair of 'ands – you're a wonder.'

MARIA (*acidly*): Well, I don't think I want a wonder here, Mrs Northrop. I'll pay you what I owe you tonight, and then you needn't come again.

MRS NORTHROP (*bridling*): Ho, I see – that's it, is it?

MARIA: Yes, it is. I don't consider you satisfactory.

CLARA: I should think not!

MRS NORTHROP (*annoyed*): Who's asking you to pass remarks? (*To Maria*.) And don't think I want to come 'ere again. Me 'usband wouldn't let me, anyhow, when he 'ears what I 'ave to tell him. We've always kept ourselves respectable.

MARIA: And what does that mean?

CLARA: Don't encourage her impudence.

MRS NORTHROP: An' *you* mind your own interference. (*To Maria*.) I was beginning' to feel sorry for you – but now—

MARIA (*coldly*): I don't know what you're talking about.

CLARA: What's she got in that bag?

MRS NORTHROP (*angrily*): I've got me old boots an' apron an' cleanin' stuff in this bag—

MARIA: I can see two bottles there—

MRS NORTHROP (*angrily*): Well, what if you can? D'you think you're the only folk i' Cleckleywyke who can buy summat to sup? If you must know, these is two stout empties I'm taking away 'cos they belong to me – bought an' paid for by me at Jackson's off-licence an' if you don't believe me go an' ask 'em.

MARIA (*stopping Clara from bursting in*): No, Clara, let her alone – we've had enough. (*To Mrs Northrop, rather haughtily.*) It's twenty-four shillings altogether, isn't it?

MRS NORTHROP (*aggressively*): No, it isn't. It's twenty-five and six – if I never speak another word.

MARIA (*going for her purse on side-table*): All right then, twenty-five and six, but I'm going to take something off for that dish you broke—

MRS NORTHROP (*angrily*): You won't take a damned ha'penny off!

CLARA: Language now as well as back-answers!

MARIA (*giving Mrs Northrop a sovereign*): Here's a pound and that's all you'll get.

MRS NORTHROP (*angrily*): I won't 'ave it. I won't 'ave it.

MARIA (*leaving it on nearest table to Mrs Northrop*): There it is, Mrs Northrop, and it's all you'll get. (*Sitting down in stately fashion and turning to Clara.*) Let's see, Clara, what were you saying? (*All three women now ignore Mrs Northrop, which makes her angrier than ever.*)

MRS NORTHROP (*drowning any possible conversation*): An' don't sit there tryin' to look like duchesses, 'cos I've lived round 'ere too long an' I know too much about yer. Tryin' to swank! Why— (*pointing to Maria*) I remember you when you were Maria Fawcett an' you were nobbut a burler and mender at Barkinson's afore you took up wi' Joe Helliwell an' he were nobbut a woolsorter i' them days. And as for you— (*pointing to Clara*) I remember time when you were weighin' out apples an' potatoes in your father's greengrocer's shop, corner o' Park Road, an' a mucky little shop it wor an' all—

MARIA (*rising, angrily*): I'll fetch my husband.

MRS NORTHROP: He isn't your husband. I was goin' to say I'm as good as you, but fact is I'm a damn sight better, 'cos I'm a respectable married woman an' that's more than any o' you can say—

CLARA (*angrily*): Get a policeman.

MRS NORTHROP (*derisively*): Get a policeman! Get a dozen, an' they'll all 'ave a good laugh when they 'ear what I 'ave to tell 'em. Not one o' you properly married at all. I 'eard that organist o' yours tellin' your 'usbands – if I can call 'em your 'usbands. I wor just be'ind t'door – an' this lot wor too good to miss – better than a turn at t'Empire.

CLARA (*angrily*): I don't believe a word of it.

MRS NORTHROP: Please yourself. But 'e give 'em a letter, an' that's why they went down to t'club to talk it over – an' I can't say I blame 'em 'cos they've plenty to talk over. An' by gow, so 'ave you three. It's about time yer thought o' getting wed, isn't it?

They stare in silence. She gives them a triumphant look, then picks up her sovereign.

And now you owe me another five an' six at least – an' if you've any sense you'll see I get it – but I can't stop no longer 'cos I've said I meet me 'usband down at *'Are an' 'Ounds*, 'cos they're 'aving a draw for a goose for Cleckley-wyke Tide an' we've three tickets – so I'll say *good night*.

She bangs the door. The three women stare at each other in consternation.

MARIA: That's why they were so queer. I knew there was something.

CLARA (*bitterly*): The daft blockheads!

ANNIE suddenly begins laughing.

CLARA: Oh – for goodness' sake, Annie Parker!

ANNIE (*still laughing*): I'm not Annie Parker. And it all sounds so silly.

MARIA (*indignantly*): Silly! What's silly about it?

CLARA (*bitterly*): Serves me right for ever bothering with anybody so gormless. Isn't this Herbert Soppitt all over! Couldn't even get us married right!

MARIA (*looking distressed*): But – Clara, Annie – this is *awful*! What are we going to do?

CLARA: I know what we're *not* going to do – and that's play *Newmarket*. (*Begins putting things away, helped by other two.*)

ANNIE: Eee – we'll look awfully silly lining up at Lane End Chapel again to get married, won't we?

CLARA (*angrily*): Oh – for goodness' sake—!

MARIA (*bitterly*): Better tell them three daftheads in t'dining-room to come in now.

CLARA: No, just a minute.

MARIA: What for?

CLARA: 'Cos I want to think, an' very sight of Herbert'll make me that mad I won't be able to think. (*Ponders a moment.*) Now if nobody knew but us, it wouldn't matter so much.

MARIA: But that fool of a parson knows—

CLARA: And the organist knows—

ANNIE: And your Mrs Northrop knows – don't forget that – and you wouldn't pay her that five-and-six—

MARIA: Here, one o' them men must fetch her back.

CLARA: I should think so. Why, if people get to know about this – we're – we're—

RUBY (*looking in, announcing loudly*): Yorkshire Argus.

CLARA (*in a panic*): We don't want any *Yorkshire Argus* here – or God knows where we'll be—

> She is interrupted by the entrance of FRED DYSON, *who has had some drinks and is pleased with himself.*

DYSON (*very heartily*): Well, here we are again. At least I am. Fred Dyson – *Yorkshire Argus*. Mrs Helliwell?

MARIA (*rather faintly*): Yes.

DYSON (*same tone*): And Mrs Albert Parker and Mrs Soppitt – three lucky ladies, eh?

> They are looking anything but fortunate.

DYSON: Now, you'd never guess my trouble.

ANNIE (*who can't resist it*): You'd never guess ours, either.

MARIA (*hastily*): Shut up, Annie. What were you saying, Mr Dyson?

DYSON: I've gone and lost our photographer – Henry Ormonroyd. Brought him with me here earlier on, then we went back to the Lion, where he'd met an old pal. I left 'em, singing *Larboard Watch* in the tap-room, not twenty minutes since, went into the private bar five minutes afterwards, couldn't find old Henry anywhere, so thought he must have come up here. By the way, where's the party?

ANNIE: This is it.

MARIA (*hastily*): Shut up, Annie. (*Rather desperately, to Dyson.*) You see, my husband – Alderman Helliwell – you know him of course?

DYSON (*heartily*): Certainly. He's quite a public figure, these days. That's why the *Argus* sent me up here tonight – when he told 'em you were all celebrating your silver wedding—

CLARA (*unpleasantly*): Oh – he suggested your coming here, did he?

DYSON: He did.

CLARA (*unpleasantly*): He would!

MARIA: Well, he didn't know then – what – I mean— (*Her voice alters and dies away.*)

DYSON: Our readers 'ud like to know all about this affair.

CLARA (*grimly*): An' I'll bet they would!

MARIA: Now 'ave a bit o' sense, Clara—

CLARA (*quickly*): Why, you nearly gave it away—

ANNIE (*coming in*): What on earth are you saying, you two? (*Smiles at Dyson, who is looking rather mystified.*) It's all right, Mr Dyson. What Mrs Helliwell was going to say was that there was only just us six, y'know. It wasn't a real party. Just a little – er – private – er – sort of – you know.

DYSON (*looking about him, thirstily*): I know. Just a cosy little do – with – er – a few drinks.

MARIA: That's it.

DYSON: A few drinks – and – er – cigars – and – er so on.
But they do not take the hint, so now he pulls out pencil and bit
of paper.

Now, Mrs Helliwell, wouldn't you like to tell our readers just
what your feelings are now that you're celebrating twenty-
five years of happy marriage?

MARIA (*her face working*): I – er – I – er—

DYSON: You needn't be shy, Mrs Helliwell. Now, come
on.

To his astonishment, MARIA *suddenly bursts into tears, and*
then hurries out of the room.

CLARA (*reproachfully*): Now, look what you've done, young
man.

DYSON (*astonished*): Nay, dash it – what have I done? I only
asked her—

ANNIE (*hastily*): She's a bit upset tonight – you know, what
with all the excitement. It's no use your staying now – you'd
better go and find your photographer.

CLARA (*angrily*): Now, Annie, for goodness' sake! We want
no photographers here.

ANNIE (*to Dyson*): That's all right. She's upset too. Now you
just pop off.

ANNIE *almost marches* DYSON *to the door and sees him*
through it. We hear him go out. CLARA *sits breathing very hard.*
ANNIE *returns, leaving door open behind her.*

ANNIE: Well, we're rid of him.

CLARA: For how long?

ANNIE (*annoyed*): You can't sit there, Clara, just saying: 'For
how long?' as if you're paying me to manage this business.
If we want it kept quiet, we'll have to stir ourselves and not
sit about shouting and nearly giving it all away as you and
Maria did when that chap was here.

CLARA (*bitterly*): If we hadn't said we'd marry a set o'
numskulls, this would never 'ave happened. If my poor
mother was alive to see this day—

MARIA *returns, blowing her nose and sits down miserably.*

MARIA (*unhappily*): I'm sorry – Clara, Annie – but I just couldn't help it. When he asked me that question, something turned right over inside – an' next minute I was crying.

CLARA (*severely*): Well, crying's not going to get us out of this mess.

ANNIE (*sharply*): You're never satisfied, Clara. First you go on at me for laughing and now you blame poor Maria for crying—

CLARA (*loudly, sharply*): Well, what do you want to go laughing an' crying for? What do you think this is? *Uncle Tom's Cabin?*

MARIA: They're coming in.

The women sit back, grimly waiting. HELLIWELL, PARKER, SOPPITT *enter, and the women look at them.*

PARKER (*uneasily*): Who was that?

No reply. He exchanges a glance with Soppitt and Helliwell.
I said, who was it came just then?

CLARA (*suddenly, fiercely*): *Yorkshire Argus!*

PARKER (*resigned tone*): They know.

ANNIE (*sharply*): Course we know.

HELLIWELL *looks at them, then makes for the door again.*

MARIA: And where are you going?

HELLIWELL: To fetch t'whisky.

MARIA: And is whisky going to 'elp us?

HELLIWELL: I don't know about you, but it'll help me. (*Goes out.*)

MARIA (*hopefully*): It's not all a tale, is it?

PARKER: No, it's right enough. We put case to a chap at club – no names, of course – and he said it 'ad 'appened a few times – when a young parson thought he was qualified to marry folk – an it turned out he wasn't. But of course it 'asn't happened often.

CLARA: No, but it has to 'appen to *us*. (*Fiercely to Soppitt.*) I blame you for this.

SOPPITT (*unhappily to Parker*): Didn't I tell you she would?

CLARA (*sharply*): *She!* Who's *she?* The cat? Just remember you're talking about your own wife.

PARKER: Ah – but you see, he isn't – not now.

CLARA (*angrily*): Now, stop that, Albert Parker.

    HELLIWELL *returns with large tray, with whisky, soda and glasses.*

HELLIWELL: Any lady like a drop?

MARIA: State I'm in now, it 'ud choke me.

    The other women shake their heads scornfully.

HELLIWELL: Albert?

PARKER: Thanks, I think I will, Joe. (*Goes to him.*)

HELLIWELL (*busy with drinks*): 'Erbert?

CLARA (*quickly*): He mustn't 'ave any.

HELLIWELL: *'Erbert?*

CLARA (*confidently*): You 'eard what I said, Herbert. You're not to 'ave any.

SOPPITT (*the rebel now*): Thanks, Joe, just a drop

    He goes up, looks at his wife as he takes his glass and drinks, then comes away, still looking at her, while she glares at him.

HELLIWELL: 'Ere, but I'd never ha' thought young Forbes ud have gone back on his word like that, when he promised solemnly not to tell another soul.

MARIA: But he didn't tell us.

HELLIWELL (*staggered*): Eh? (*Exchanges alarmed glance with other men.*) Who did then?

MARIA: Charwoman – Mrs Northrop. She 'eard you, behind that door.

HELLIWELL (*alarmed*): 'Ere, where is she?

MARIA: Gone.

ANNIE (*with some malice*): Maria's just given her the push.

PARKER (*angrily*): If she's gone off with this news you just might as well play it on Town Hall chimes.

HELLIWELL (*angrily*): Why didn't you say so at first? If this woman gets round wi' this tale about us, we'll never live it down. Did she go 'ome?

ANNIE: No, to the Hare and Hounds.

HELLIWELL (*masterfully*): Herbert, swallow that whisky quick – an' nip down to t'Hare an' Hounds as fast as you can go, an' bring her back—

SOPPITT: But I don't know her.

HELLIWELL: Nay, damn it, you saw her in here, not an hour since—

SOPPITT: An' she doesn't know me.

HELLIWELL: Now, don't make difficulties, Herbert. Off you go. (*Moves him towards conservatory.*) And bring her back as fast as you can and promise her owt she asks so long as you get back. (*He is now outside, shouting.*) An' make haste. We're depending on you.

HELLIWELL *returns, blowing, carrying Soppitt's glass. He is about to drink out of this when he remembers, so takes and drinks from his own, then breathes noisily and mops his brow. They are all quiet for a moment.*

You know, Albert lad, it feels quite peculiar to me.

PARKER: What does?

HELLIWELL: This – not being married.

MARIA (*rising solemn*): Joe Helliwell, 'ow can you stand there an' say a thing like that?

CLARA: ⎱ He ought to be ashamed of himself.
ANNIE: ⎰ I'm surprised at you, Joe.

HELLIWELL (*bewildered*): What – what are you talking about?

MARIA (*solemnly*): After twenty-five years together. Haven't I been a good wife to you, Joe Helliwell?

HELLIWELL: Well, I'm not complaining, am I?

PARKER (*tactlessly*): You've been the *same* as a good wife to him, Maria.

MARIA (*furiously*): The *same*! I haven't been the same as a good wife, I've been a good wife, let me tell you, Albert Parker.

ANNIE: ⎱ Nay, Albert!
CLARA: ⎰ (*angrily to Parker*): I never 'eard such silly talk.

PARKER (*aggressively*): Oh – an' what's silly about it, eh?

CLARA: Everything.

HELLIWELL (*tactlessly*): Nay, but when you come to think of it – Albert's right.

PARKER (*solemn and fatuous*): We must face facts. Now, Maria, you might *feel* married to him—

MARIA (*scornfully*): *I might feel married to him!* If you'd had twenty-five years of him, you wouldn't talk about *might*. Haven't I—

HELLIWELL (*cutting in noisily*): 'Ere, steady on, steady on – with your *twenty-five years of 'im*. Talking about me as if I were a dose o' typhoid fever.

MARIA (*loudly*): I'm not, Joe. All I'm saying is—

PARKER (*still louder*): Now let me finish what I started to say. I said – you might *feel* married to him – but strictly speaking – and in the eyes of the law – the fact is, you're *not* married to him. We're none of us married.

CLARA (*bitterly*): Some o' t'neighbours ha' missed it. Couldn't you shout it louder?

PARKER: I wasn't that loud.

HELLIWELL (*reproachfully*): You were bawling your 'ead off.

ANNIE: Yes, you were.

MARIA (*reproachfully*): You don't know who's listening. I'm surprised you haven't more sense, Albert.

PARKER (*irritably*): All right, all right, all right. But we shan't get anywhere till we face facts. It's not our fault, but our misfortune.

MARIA: I don't know so much about that either.

HELLIWELL: Oh? (*To Albert.*) Goin' to blame us now.

MARIA: Well, an' why not?

HELLIWELL (*irritably*): Nay, damn it – it wasn't *our* fault.

MARIA: If a chap asks me to marry him and then he takes me to chapel and puts me in front of a parson, I expect parson to be a real one an' not just somebody dressed up.

HELLIWELL: Well, don't I?

MARIA: You should ha' found out.

HELLIWELL: Talk sense! 'Ow could I know he wasn't properly qualified?

MARIA (*sneering*): Well, it's funny it's got to 'appen to us, isn't it?

PARKER: But that's what I say – it's not our fault, it's our misfortune. It's no use blaming anybody. Just couldn't be 'elped. But fact remains – we're—

CLARA (*interrupting angrily*): If you say it again, Albert Parker, I'll throw something at yer. You needn't go on and on about it.

MARIA (*bitterly*): Mostly at top o' your voice.

PARKER (*with air of wounded dignity*): Say no more. I've finished. (*Turns his back on them.*)

All three women look at him disgustedly. MARIA *now turns to* JOE.

MARIA: But, Joe, you're not going to tell me you feel different – just because of this – this accident?

JOE (*solemnly*): I won't tell you a lie, love. I can't help it, but ever since I've known I'm not married I've felt *most peculiar.*

MARIA (*rising, sudden temper*): Oo, I could knock your fat head off.

MARIA goes hurriedly to the door, making sobbing noises on the way, and hurries out.

ANNIE (*following her*): Oh – poor Maria!

ANNIE goes out, closing door.

CLARA: Well, I 'ope you're pleased with yourself now.

HELLIWELL (*sententiously*): Never interfere between 'usband and wife.

CLARA: You just said you weren't 'usband an' wife.

HELLIWELL (*angrily*): 'Ere, if I'm going to argue with a woman it might as well be the one I live with.

HELLIWELL hurries out. A silence. PARKER *remains sulky and detached.*

CLARA (*after pause*): Well, after all these ructions, another glass o' port wouldn't do me any 'arm. (*Waits, then as there is no move from Parker.*) Thank you very much. (*Rises, with dignity, to help herself.*) Nice manners we're being shown, I must say. (*Fills her glass.*) I said *nice manners*, Councillor Albert Parker!

PARKER (*turning angrily*): Now if I were poor Herbert Soppitt, I'd think twice before I asked you to marry me again.

CLARA (*just going to drink*): *Ask me again!* There'll be no asking. Herbert Soppitt's my husband – an' he stays my husband.

PARKER: In the eyes of the law—

CLARA (*cutting in ruthlessly*): You said that before. But let me tell you, in the sight of Heaven Herbert and me's been married for twenty-five years.

PARKER (*triumphantly*): And there you're wrong again, because in the sight of Heaven nobody's married at all—

HELLIWELL *pops his head in, looking worried.*

HELLIWELL: Just come in the dining-room a minute, Albert. We're having a bit of an argument—

PARKER: Yes, Joe.

HELLIWELL *disappears.* PARKER *goes out, leaving door a little open.* CLARA, *left alone, finishes her port, then picks up the old photograph and glares with contempt at the figures on it. A house bell can be heard ringing distantly now.*

CLARA (*muttering her profound contempt at the figures in the photograph*): Yer silly young softheads! (*Bangs it down in some prominent place, face up.*)

RUBY *now looks in.*

RUBY: Mrs Soppitt—

CLARA (*rather eagerly*): Yes?

RUBY: Mrs Helliwell says will you go into t' dining-room.

As CLARA *moves quickly towards door,* RUBY *adds coolly.*

Aaa – they're fratchin' like mad.

CLARA *goes out quickly, followed by* RUBY. *We hear in distance sound of door opening, the voices of the three in the dining-room noisily raised in argument, the shutting of the door then a moment's silence. Then several sharp rings at the front door. After a moment,* RUBY'S *voice off, but coming nearer.*

(*Off.*) Yes, I know . . . All right . . . 'Ere, mind them things . . . This way . . .

RUBY *ushers in* ORMONROYD, *who is carrying his camera, etc., and is now very ripe.*

ORMONROYD (*advances into room and looks about him with great care, then returns to Ruby*): Nobody here. (*Gives another glance to make sure.*) Nobody at all.

RUBY: They'll all be back again soon. They're mostly in dining-room – fratchin'.

ORMONROYD: What – on a festive occasion like this?

RUBY: That's right.

ORMONROYD: Well, it just shows you what human nature is. Human nature! T-t-t-t-t-t. I'll bet if it had been a funeral – they'd have all been in here, laughing their heads off. (*He goes over and looks closely at the cigars.*) There isn't such a thing as a cigar here, is there?

RUBY: Yes, yer looking at 'em. D'you want one? 'Ere. (*As he lights it.*) Me mother says if God had intended men to smoke He'd have put chimneys in their heads.

ORMONROYD: Tell your mother from me that if God had intended men to wear collars He'd have put collar studs at back of their necks. (*Stares at her.*) What are you bobbing up an' down like that for?

RUBY: I'm not bobbing up an' down. It's you. (*Laughs and regards him critically.*) You're a bit tiddly, aren't yer?

ORMONROYD (*horror-struck*): Tidd-ldly?

RUBY: Yes. Squiffy.

ORMONROYD (*surveying her mistily*): What an ex't'rornry idea! You seem to me a mos' ex't'rornry sort of – little – well, I dunno, really – what's your name?

RUBY: Ruby Birtle.

ORMONROYD (*tasting it*): Umm – Ruby—

RUBY: All right, I know it's a silly daft name; you can't tell me nowt about Ruby I 'aven't been told already – so don't try.

ORMONROYD (*solemnly*): Ruby, I think you're quite ex't'rornry. How old are you?

RUBY (*quickly*): Fifteen – how old are you?

ORMONROYD (*waving a hand, vaguely*): Thousands of years, thousands and thousands of years.

RUBY (*coolly*): You look to me about seventy.

ORMONROYD (*horrified*): *Seventy!* I'm fifty-four.

RUBY (*severely*): Then you've been neglectin' yerself.

ORMONROYD *looks at her, breathing hard and noisily.*

Too much liftin' o' t' elbow.

ORMONROYD (*after indignant pause*): Do you ever read the *Police News?*

RUBY: Yes. I like it. All 'orrible murders.

ORMONROYD: Then you must have seen them pictures of women who've been chopped up by their husbands—

RUBY (*with gusto*): Yes – with bloody 'atchets.

ORMONROYD (*impressively*): Well, if you don't look out, Ruby, you'll grow up to be one of them women. (*Wanders away and then notices and takes up old photograph.*)

RUBY (*looking at it*): Aaaaa! – don't they look soft? (*Looks suspiciously at him, dubiously.*) How d'you mean – one o' them women?

ORMONROYD: Don't you bother about that, Ruby; you've plenty of time yet.

RUBY (*puzzled*): Time for what?

ORMONROYD (*intent on his art now*): Now what I'm going to do – is to take a flashlight group of the three couples – just as they were in the old photograph. Now – let me see— *Very solemnly and elaborately he sets up his camera.*)

RUBY (*who has been thinking*): 'Ere, d'you mean I've plenty of time yet to grow up an' then be chopped up?

ORMONROYD (*absently*): Yes.

RUBY (*persistently*): But what would 'e want to chop me up for?

ORMONROYD: Now you sit there a minute.

RUBY: I said, what would 'e want to chop me up for?

ORMONROYD (*putting her into a chair and patting her shoulder*): Perhaps you might find one who wouldn't, but you'll have to be careful. Now you stay there, Ruby.

RUBY (*hopefully*): Are yer goin' to take my photo?

ORMONROYD (*grimly*): Not for a few years – yet— (*Is now fiddling with his camera.*)

RUBY (*after thoughtful pause*): D'you mean you're waiting for me to be chopped up? (*Cheerfully, not reproachfully.*) Eeeee! – you've got a right nasty mind, 'aven't you? (*A pause.*) Are *you* married?

ORMONROYD: Yes.

RUBY: Yer wife doesn't seem to take much interest in yer.

ORMONROYD: How do you know?

RUBY: Well, I'll bet yer clothes hasn't been brushed for a month. (*Going on cheerfully.*) Yer could almost make a meal off yer waistcoat – there's so much egg on it. (*After pause.*) Why doesn't she tidy you up a bit?

ORMONROYD (*busy with his preparations*): Because she's not here to do it.

RUBY: Doesn't she live with yer?

ORMONROYD (*stopping to stare at her, with dignity*): Is it – er – essential – you should know all about my – er – private affairs?

RUBY: Go on, yer might as well tell me. Where is she?

ORMONROYD: Mrs Ormonroyd at present is – er – helping her sister to run a boarding-house called *Palm View* – though the only palm you see there is the one my sister-in-law holds out.

RUBY: Where? Blackpool?

ORMONROYD: Not likely. There's a place you go to live in – not to die in. No, they're at Torquay. (*With profound scorn.*) *Torquay!*

RUBY (*impressed*): That's right down South, isn't it?

ORMONROYD (*with mock pompousness*): Yes, my girl, Torquay is on the South Coast of Devonshire. It is sheltered from the northerly and easterly winds, is open to the warm sea breezes from the South, and so is a favourite all-year-round resort of many delicate and refined persons of genteel society. In other words, it's a damned miserable hole.

(*Surveys his arrangements with satisfaction.*) There we are, all
ready for the three happy couples.

RUBY (*sceptically*): Did yer say 'appy?

ORMONROYD: Why not?

RUBY: Well, for a start, go an' listen to them four in t' dining-
room.

ORMONROYD (*beginning solemnly*): Believe me, Rosie—

RUBY (*sharply*): Ruby.

ORMONROYD: Ruby. Believe me, you're still too young to
understand.

RUBY: I've 'eard that afore, but nobody ever tells what it is I'm
too young to understand. An' for years me brother kept
rabbits.

ORMONROYD (*solemnly but vaguely*): It's not a question of
rabbits – thank God! But marriage – marriage – well, it's a
very peculiar thing. There's parts of it I never much cared
about myself.

RUBY: Which parts?

ORMONROYD: Well – now I'm a man who likes a bit o'
company. An' I like an occasional friendly glass. I'll admit
it – I like an occasional friendly glass.

RUBY: It 'ud be all t'same if you didn't admit it. We could
tell. (*Sniffs.*)

ORMONROYD: If these three couples here have been married
for twenty-five years and – er – they're still sticking it, well,
then I can call 'em three happy couples, an' I won't listen to
you or anybody else saying they're not. No, I won't have it.
And if you or anybody else says 'Drink their health' I say
'Certainly, certainly, with pleasure—' (*Gives himself a
whisky with remarkable speed.*) Wouldn't dare to refuse, 'coz
it would be dead against my principles. Their very good
health. (*Takes an enormous drink.*)

RUBY: Eeee! – you are goin' to be tiddly.

ORMONROYD (*ignoring this, if he heard it, and very mellow and
sentimental now*): Ah – yes. To be together – side-by-side –
through all life's sunshine and storms – hand-in-hand – in

good times and bad ones – with always a loving smile—
Waving hand with cigar in.)

RUBY (*coldly*): Mind yer cigar!

ORMONROYD: In sickness and in health – rich or poor – still
together – side-by-side – hand-in-hand – through all life's
sunshine and storms—

RUBY (*quickly*): You said that once.

ORMONROYD: Oh – yes – it's a wonderful – it's a bee-yutiful
thing—

RUBY: What is?

ORMONROYD: *What is!* Lord help us – like talking to a little
crocodile! I say – that it's a wonderful and bee-yutiful thing
to go through good times and bad ones – always together –
always with a loving smile—

RUBY: Side-by-side – an' 'and-in-'and—

ORMONROYD: Yes, and that's what I say.

RUBY: Then there must be summat wrong wi' me 'cos when
I've tried goin' side-by-side an' 'and-in-'and even for twenty
minutes I've 'ad more than I want.

ORMONROYD (*staring at her*): Extr'ord'n'ry! What's your
name?

RUBY: It's still Ruby Birtle.

ORMONROYD: Well, haven't you had a home?

RUBY: Course I've 'ad a home. Why?

ORMONROYD: You talk as if you'd been brought up in a
tramshed. No sentiment. No tender feeling. No – no –
poetry—

RUBY (*indignantly*): Go on. I know Poetry. We learnt it at
school. 'Ere—

RUBY *recites, as* ORMONROYD *sits.*

They grew in beauty side by side,
    They filled one home with glee;
Their graves are severed, far an' wide,
    By mount and stream and sea.

The same fond mother bent at night
   O'er each fair sleeping brow;
She 'ad each folder flower in sight —
   Where are those dreamers now?

One 'midst the forest of the west,
   By a dark stream is laid –
The Indian knows his place of rest
   Far—

     RUBY *hesitates.* CLARA *enters quietly and stares at her in astonishment.* RUBY *gives her one startled look, then concludes hurriedly.*

     – Far in the cedar shade.

     RUBY *hurries out.* CLARA *stands in Ruby's place.* ORMONROYD, *who has turned away and closed his eyes, now turns and opens them, astonished to see Clara there.*

ORMONROYD (*bewildered*): Now I call that most peculiar, *most* peculiar. I don't think I'm very well tonight—

CLARA (*same tone as Ruby used*): You're a bit tiddly, aren't you?

ORMONROYD: Things aren't rightly in their place, if you know what I mean. But I'll get it.

CLARA: Who are you, and what are you doing here?

ORMONROYD (*still dazed*): Henry Ormonroyd – *Yorkshire Argus* – take picture – silver wedding group—

CLARA (*firmly*): There's no silver wedding group'll be taken *here* tonight.

ORMONROYD: Have I come to t'wrong house?

CLARA (*firmly*): Yes.

ORMONROYD: Excuse me. (*Moving to door, which opens to admit Annie.*)

ANNIE: Who's this?

ORMONROYD (*hastily confused*): Nobody, nobody – I'll get it all straightened out in a minute – now give me time—

     ORMONROYD *goes out.*

ANNIE: Isn't he the photographer?

CLARA (*bitterly*): Yes, an' he's drunk, an' when I come in, Maria's servant's reciting poetry to him, an' God knows what's become of Herbert an' Albert an' that Mrs Northrop an' (*angrily*) I'm fast losing my patience, I'm fast losing my patience—

ANNIE: Now, Clara—

> MARIA *enters, rather wearily.*

MARIA: I can't knock any sense at all into Joe. Where's Herbert?

CLARA (*grimly*): Still looking for that Mrs Northrop.

> *Front door bell rings.*

Somebody else here now.

MARIA: Well, don't carry on like that, Clara. I didn't ask 'em to come, whoever it is.

CLARA: If you didn't, I'll bet Joe did. With his *Yorkshire Argus*!

> RUBY *enters, rather mysteriously.*

MARIA: Well, Ruby, who is it?

RUBY (*lowering voice*): It's a woman.

CLARA (*hastily*): What woman?

MARIA: Now, Clara! (*To Ruby.*) What sort of woman? Who is it?

RUBY (*coming in, confidentially*): I don't know. But she doesn't look up to much to me. Paint on her face. An' I believe her 'air's dyed.

> *The three women look at each other.*

CLARA (*primly*): We don't want that sort o' woman here, Maria.

MARIA: Course we don't – but— (*Hesitates.*)

ANNIE: You'll have to see what she wants, Maria. It might be something to do with – y'know – this business.

CLARA (*angrily*): How could it be?

ANNIE: Well, you never know, do yer?

CLARA: Let Joe see what she wants.

MARIA: Oh – no – state of mind Joe's in, *I'd* better see her. Ask her to come in, Ruby – and – er – you needn't bother Mr Helliwell just now.

RUBY *goes out. The three women settle themselves, rather anxiously.* RUBY *ushers in* LOTTIE, *who enters smiling broadly.* MARIA *rises, the other two remaining seated.*

MARIA (*nervously*): Good evening.

LOTTIE: Good evening.

MARIA (*step down*): Did you want to see me?

LOTTIE (*coolly*): No, not particularly. (*She sits down, calmly, and looks about her.*)

The other three women exchange puzzled glances.

MARIA: Er – I don't think I got your name.

LOTTIE: No. You didn't get it because I didn't give it. But I'm Miss Lottie Grady.

MARIA (*with dignity*): And I'm Mrs Helliwell.

LOTTIE (*shaking her head*): No, if we're all going to be on our dignity, let's get it *right.* You're not Mrs Helliwell. You're Miss Maria Fawcett.

CLARA (*as Maria is too stunned to speak*): Now just a minute—

LOTTIE (*turning to her, with mock sweetness*): Miss Clara Gawthorpe, isn't it? Gawthorpe's, Greengrocer's, corner of Park Road. (*Turning to Annie.*) I'm afraid I don't know *your* maiden name—

ANNIE: I'm Mrs Parker to you.

LOTTIE: Please yourself. I don't care. I'm *broadminded.* (*Surveying them with a smile.*)

CLARA (*angrily*): I suppose that Mrs Northrop's been talking to you.

LOTTIE: Certainly. Met in the old Hare and Hounds, where I used to work. She's an old friend of mine.

CLARA (*angrily*): If you've come 'ere to get money out of us—

LOTTIE: Who said anything about money?

MARIA: Well, you must have some idea in coming to see us.

LOTTIE (*coolly*): Oh – I didn't come here to see any of you three.

ANNIE: Well, who did you come to see then?

LOTTIE (*smiling*): A gentleman friend, love.

CLARA (*angrily*): *Gentleman friend! You*'ll find none o' your gentleman friends in *this house*, will she, Maria?

MARIA (*indignantly*): I should think not!

ANNIE: Just a minute, Clara. I'd like to hear a bit more about this.

LOTTIE: Very sensible of you. You see, if a gentleman friend gets fond of me – then tells me – more than once – that if he wasn't married already, he'd marry me—

CLARA (*grimly*): Well, go on.

LOTTIE: Well – then I suddenly find out that he isn't married already, after all, then you can't blame me – can you? – if I'd like to know if he's still in the same mind. (*Beams upon them, while they look at each other in growing consternation.*)

CLARA (*astounded*): Well, I'll be hanged.

ANNIE: Now we *are* getting to know something.

MARIA (*flustered*): Clara – Annie. (*Pause. Suddenly to Lottie.*) Who was it?

    Front door bell rings.

ANNIE: Just a minute, Maria, there's somebody else here now.

CLARA (*angrily*): Oh – for goodness' sake – can't you keep 'em out?

RUBY (*appearing, importantly*): The Rever-ent Clem-ent Mer-cer!

    All three wives look startled, as MERCER, *a large grave clergyman, enters, and* RUBY *retires.*

MERCER (*sympathetically*): Mrs Helliwell?

MARIA (*faintly*): Yes?

MERCER (*taking her hand a moment*): Now, Mrs Helliwell, although you're not a member of my congregation, I want you to realize that I feel it my duty to give you any help I can.

MARIA (*confused*): I'm afraid – I don't understand – Mr Mercer.

MERCER: Now, now, Mrs Helliwell, don't worry. Let's take everything calmly. May I sit down? (*Takes chair and brings it down.*)

MERCER *sits down, smiling at them.* MARIA *sits.*

ANNIE: Did somebody ask you to come here?

MERCER: Yes, madam. A working man I know called Northrop stopped me in the street and told me to go at once to Alderman Helliwell's house as a clergyman's presence was urgently required here. So here I am – entirely at your service.

LOTTIE, *in danger of exploding, rises and goes quickly towards conservatory, where she stands with her back to the others.* MERCER *gives her a puzzled glance, then turns to the other three.*

Now what is it? Not, I hope, a really dangerous illness?

MARIA (*blankly*): No.

MERCER (*rather puzzled*): Ah! – I hurried because I thought there might be. But perhaps you feel some younger member of your family is in urgent need of spiritual guidance. An erring son or daughter?

A noise from LOTTIE.

CLARA (*forcefully*): No.

MERCER (*puzzled*): I beg your pardon?

CLARA: I just said *No.* I mean, there aren't any erring sons and daughters. Just husbands, that's all.

MERCER (*rises*): Husbands?

LOTTIE *suddenly bursts into a peal of laughter, turning towards them.* MERCER *looks puzzled at her.*

LOTTIE (*laughing*): You've got it all wrong.

MERCER (*rather annoyed*): Really! I don't see—

LOTTIE: I think they want you to marry 'em.

MERCER (*looking astounded*): *Marry them!*

ANNIE (*rising, with spirit*): 'Ere, Maria, come on, do something. (*To Mercer.*) You'd better talk to Mr Helliwell—

MARIA (*who has risen*): He's in the dining-room – just across— (*Almost leading him out.*) Ask him if he thinks you can do anything for us— (*Now outside room.*) Just in there – that's right—

CLARA (*to Lottie*): Which one was it?

MARIA *returns, flustered, shutting door, as* LOTTIE *returns to her seat, still smiling.*

LOTTIE: I think you missed a chance there – at least, two of you did.

MARIA: Two of us!

LOTTIE: Well, you remember what I told you? (*Smiling reminiscently.*) I'd known him here in Cleckleywyke, but it was at Blackpool we really got going. He said he was feeling lonely – and you know what men are, when they think they're feeling lonely, specially at Blackpool.

CLARA (*hastily*): It couldn't have been Herbert. He's never been to Blackpool without me.

ANNIE: Yes, he has, Clara. Don't you remember – about four years since—?

CLARA (*thunderstruck*): And he said he hadn't a minute away from that Conference. I'll never believe another word he says. But your Albert was with him that time.

ANNIE (*grimly*): I know he was.

MARIA: So was Joe. Said he needed a change.

LOTTIE (*sweetly*): Well, we all like a change, don't we?

SOPPITT *enters, rather hesitantly.* CLARA *sees him first.*

CLARA (*sharply*): Now, Herbert Soppitt—

SOPPITT: Yes Clara?

LOTTIE (*going to him*): Well, Herbert, how are you these days? (*Playfully.*) You haven't forgotten me, have you?

SOPPITT: Forgotten you? I'm afraid there's a mistake—

CLARA (*grimly*): Oh – there's a mistake all right.

MARIA: Now, Clara, don't be too hard on him. I expect it was only a bit o' fun.

SOPPITT: What is all this?

LOTTIE (*playfully*): Now, Herbert—

SOPPITT (*indignantly*): Don't call me Herbert.

CLARA (*angrily*): No, wait till I'm out o' t' way.

ANNIE: I expect he didn't mean it.

SOPPITT (*annoyed*): Mean *what*?

ALBERT PARKER *now enters, rather wearily.* SOPPITT *turns to him.*

I found that Mrs Northrop, Albert.

LOTTIE: Oh – hello, Albert!

PARKER (*staring at her*): How d'you mean – *Hello, Albert!*

LOTTIE (*playfully*): Now, now – Albert!

PARKER *looks at her in astonishment, then at the three women, finishing with his wife.*

ANNIE (*bitterly*): Yes, you might well look at me, Albert Parker. You and your cheap holiday at Blackpool! I only hope you spent more on her than you've ever done on me.

PARKER (*vehemently*): Spent more on *her*? I've never set eyes on her before. *Who is she?*

ANNIE *and* CLARA *now look at one another, then at* MARIA, *who looks at them in growing consternation.*

MARIA: I don't believe it. I *won't* believe it.

RUBY *looks in, excitedly.*

RUBY: There's a motor-car stopping near t'front gate.

CLARA (*shouting as* RUBY *goes*): Well, tell it to go away again

HELLIWELL *comes out of dining-room, bumping into* RUBY *as she goes out, and begins speaking early.*

HELLIWELL (*who is flustered*): What with a photographer who's drunk and a parson who's mad—! (*He sees Lottie now and visibly wilts and gasps.*) Lottie!

MARIA (*furiously*): Lottie! So it was *you*, Joe Helliwell.

HELLIWELL: Me what?

MARIA: Who said you'd marry her—

HELLIWELL (*shouting desperately*): That was only a bit o' fun

MARIA (*bitterly*): You and your bit o' fun!

RUBY (*importantly*): Mayor o' Cleckleywyke, *Yorkshire Argus Telegraph and Mercury.*

MAYOR *enters, carrying case of fish slices, with* REPORTER *behind.*

MAYOR (*pompously*): Alderman and Mrs Helliwell, the Council and Corporation of Cleckleywyke offers you their heartiest congratulations on your Silver Wedding and with them this case of silver fish slices.

He is now offering the case to MARIA, *who has suddenly sunk down on the settee and is now weeping. She waves the case away, and the bewildered* MAYOR *now offers it to* HELLIWELL, *who has been looking in exasperation between his wife,* LOTTIE *and the* MAYOR. HELLIWELL *takes the case and opens it without thinking, then seeing what is in it, in his exasperation, shouts furiously:*

An' I told yer before, Fred – I don't like fish. (*Quick curtain.*)

END OF ACT TWO

ACT THREE

Scene: As before. About a quarter of an hour later. RUBY *is tidying up the room, and also eating a large piece of pastry. She continues with her work several moments after rise of curtain, then* NANCY *makes cautious appearance at conservatory, sees that nobody but* RUBY *is there, then turns to beckon in* GERALD, *and they both come into the room.*

NANCY: What's been happening, Ruby?

RUBY: What 'asn't been 'appening! Eee – we've had some trade on what wi' one thing an' another.

NANCY (*mischievous rather than reproachful*): You see what you've done, Gerald.

RUBY: What! He didn't start it, did he? 'Cos if he did, he's got summat to answer for.

NANCY: Did – anybody ask where I was, Ruby?

RUBY: No, an' I'll bet you could stop out all night and they'd neither know nor care.

GERALD: But what *has* been happening, Ruby?

RUBY (*confidentially*): Place 'as been like a mad-'ouse this last half-hour. To start with, mayor o' Cleckleywyke's been and gone—

NANCY: The mayor?

GERALD (*amused*): Why did they want to bring the mayor into it?

RUBY: Nobody brought him. He come of his own accord – with a case o' fish things an' wearing t' chain – like a chap in a pantymime. He soon took his 'ook. But reporters didn't—

GERALD: Reporters, eh?

RUBY: Ay, an' there were plenty of 'em an' all an' they didn't want to go, neither, not like t'mayor. So Mr Helliwell an' Mr Parker took 'em into t' kitchen an' give 'em bottled ale an' for all I know they may be there yet. Mrs Helliwell's up in t' bedroom – feeling poorly – an' Mrs Soppitt's with her. Mr Soppitt an' Mrs Parker's somewhere out in garden—

NANCY: I told you there was somebody there.

RUBY: Ah, but let me finish. Now there's a woman wi' dyed 'air washing herself in t'bathroom upstairs – an' nobody knows what she wants – beyond a good wash. Down in t' dining-room there's a photographer who's right tiddly tryin' to argue with gert big parson – an' I'll bet he's makin' a rare mess – an' that'll be to do next.

Exit RUBY.

GERALD: Sounds all very confused to me.

NANCY: Yes, and I'd better slip upstairs while nobody's about. Oh – Gerald.

GERALD: Nancy!

NANCY: Do you still love me?

GERALD: Yes, Nancy – still – even after a whole hour.

They kiss. Enter SOPPITT *and* ANNIE PARKER *from conservatory.*

SOPPITT: Here. I say! You two seem very friendly!

ANNIE: I believe you were the girl he was seen with.

SOPPITT: Were you?

NANCY: Yes. We're practically engaged, you know. Only – I was frightened of saying anything yet to Uncle Joe.

SOPPITT: Well, don't start tonight—

ANNIE: Why shouldn't she? He won't be quite so pleased with himself tonight as usual – just as I know another who won't.

NANCY: Good night.

ANNIE: Good night. Why don't you go outside and say good night properly? You're only young once.

NANCY *and* GERALD *exit to conservatory.*

ANNIE: Yes, you're only young once, Herbert. D'you remember that time, just after you'd first come to Cleckleywyke, when we all went on that choir trip to Barnard Castle?

SOPPITT: I do, Annie. As a matter of fact, I fancy I was a bit sweet on you then.

ANNIE: You fancy you were! I know you were, Herbert Soppitt. Don't you remember coming back in the wagonette?

SOPPITT: Ay!

ANNIE: Those were the days!

SOPPITT: Ay!

ANNIE: Is that all you can say – Ay?

SOPPITT: No. But I might say too much.

ANNIE: I think I'd risk it for once, if I were you.

SOPPITT: And what does that mean, Annie?

ANNIE: Never you mind. But you haven't forgotten that wagonette, have you?

SOPPITT: Of course I haven't.

He has his arm round her waist. Enter CLARA.

Hello, Clara.

CLARA: How long's this been going on?

ANNIE: Now, don't be silly, Clara.

CLARA: Oh – it's me that hasn't to be silly, is it? I suppose standing there with my 'usband's arm round you bold as brass, that isn't being silly, is it? I wonder what you call that sort of behaviour, then?

SOPPITT: It was only a bit of fun.

CLARA: Oh – an' how long have you been 'aving these bits o' fun – as you call them – Herbert Soppitt?

ANNIE: You've a nasty mind, Clara.

CLARA: Well – of all the cheek and impudence! Telling me I've got a nasty mind. You must have been at it some time getting Herbert to carry on like that with you. Don't tell me he thought of it himself, I know him too well.

ANNIE: Oh – don't be so stupid, Clara. I'm going into the garden. I want some fresh air.

She goes out.

CLARA: Well, Herbert Soppitt, why don't you follow her and get some fresh air, too? Go on, don't mind me. Come here.

SOPPITT *doesn't move.*

You 'eard me. Come here!

SOPPITT: Why should I?

CLARA: Because I tell you to.

SOPPITT: I know. I heard you. But who do you think you are?

CLARA: Herbert Soppitt – you must have gone wrong in your head.

SOPPITT: No. Not me. I'm all right.

CLARA (*sharply*): You'd better go home now an' leave me to deal with this business here.

SOPPITT (*bravely*): Certainly not.

CLARA: In my opinion it's awkward with both of us here.

SOPPITT (*pause*): Well, *you* go home then!

CLARA: What did you say?

SOPPITT (*bravely*): I said, *you* go home. You are doing no good here.

Very angry now, she marches up to him and gives him a sharp slap on the cheek.

CLARA: Now then! (*Steps back and folds arms.*) Just tell me to go home again!

SOPPITT (*slowly, impressively, approaching her*): Clara, I always said that no matter what she did, I'd never lift a hand to my wife—

CLARA: I should think not indeed!

SOPPITT: But as you aren't my wife – what about this?

He gives her a sharp slap. She is astounded.

CLARA: Herbert!

SOPPITT (*commandingly*): Now sit down. (*Pointing.*)

She does not obey. In a tremendous voice of command.

Sit down!

She sits, staring at him. Then when she opens her mouth to speak:

Shut up! I want to think.

A silence, during which she still stares at him.

CLARA (*in a low voice*): I don't know what's come over you, Herbert Soppitt.

SOPPITT (*fiercely*): You don't, eh?

CLARA (*gaping at him*): No, I don't.

SOPPITT (*severely*): Well, you don't think I put up with women coming shouting and bawling at me and smacking my face, do you?

CLARA: Well – you've never gone on like this before.

SOPPITT: Yes, but then before you were my wife—

CLARA (*hastily*): I'm your wife now.

SOPPITT: Oh, no – you're not. (*Produces letter.*)

CLARA: Give me that letter!

SOPPITT: *Sit down* – and *shut up, woman!*

    Enter ALBERT PARKER.

PARKER: Where's Annie?

SOPPITT: She's out there somewhere – why don't you look for her?

CLARA: Perhaps she's hiding her face – and if you'd seen what I'd seen tonight, Albert Parker—

SOPPITT: Hold your tongue before it gets you into mischief!

CLARA: I'm only—

SOPPITT: *Shut up.*

PARKER: Here, but wait a minute – I'd like to hear a bit more about this.

SOPPITT: Then you're going to be disappointed. (*To Clara.*) You get back to Maria Helliwell, go on!

PARKER: Here, Clara, you're not going to—

SOPPITT: YOU mind your own business! (*To Clara.*) Go on – sharp.

    CLARA *exits.*

PARKER: Herbert, 'ave you been 'aving a lot to drink?

SOPPITT: I had a few, trying to find that Mrs Northrop.

PARKER: I thought as much.

SOPPITT: And I may possibly have some more, but whether I do or not, I'll please myself – just for once – and if any of you don't like it, you can lump it.

PARKER: Where did you say my wife was?

SOPPITT: She's out there in the garden.

PARKER (*disapprovingly*): What – at this time o' night? (*Looking to garden.*)

SOPPITT: Yes – and why not?

PARKER (*with dignity*): I'll tell '*er* that. I've no need to tell you. You're not my wife.

SOPPITT: No, and she isn't either. Don't forget that.

PARKER *goes to the door and calls.*

PARKER: Annie! Hey – Annie!

SOPPITT: Why don't you go out and talk to her, instead o' calling her like that – as if she were a dog or something?

PARKER: 'Cos standing about in damp grass this time o' night is bad for me. I don't want to start a running cold on top of all this. (*Calls again.*) Hey – Annie! (*Turns to Soppitt.*) I came in to 'ave a few words in private with her—

SOPPITT: Oh – I'll leave you.

PARKER: In my opinion, there's been a lot too much talk among us altogether, too much noisy 'anky-panky about this daft business. You might think we were a meeting o' t' gas committee way we've gone on so far. What's wanted is a few serious words i' private between us chaps an' our wives, an' less o' this public argy-bargy an' 'anky-panky.

ANNIE PARKER *enters through conservatory.*

Ah – so there y'are.

SOPPITT (*going*): Well, best o' luck, Annie!

PARKER (*suspiciously*): How d'you mean?

SOPPITT (*turning at door*): Hanky-panky!

He goes out.

PARKER: He's 'ad a drop too much, Herbert 'as! Comes of running round the town after that charwoman!

ANNIE (*amused*): Well, Albert?

PARKER (*pompously and complacently*): Well, Annie, I'm going to set your mind at rest.

ANNE (*demurely*): Thank you, Albert.

PARKER (*pompously and complacently*): Yes, I don't want you to be worrying. Now I think you'll admit I've always tried to do my duty as a 'usband.

ANNIE: Yes, Albert, I think you've always tried.

PARKER (*suspiciously*): What do you mean?

ANNIE (*demurely*): Why – just what you mean, Albert.

PARKER (*after another suspicious glance, returns to former tone, and is insufferably patronizing*): Of course, as nobody knows better than you, I'm in a different position altogether to what I was when I first married you—

ANNIE: When you *thought* you married me, Albert.

PARKER: Well, you know what I mean! In them days I was just plain young Albert Parker.

ANNIE: And now you're Councillor Albert Parker—

PARKER: Well, an' that's something, isn't it? And it isn't all, by a long chalk. I've got on i' business, made money, come to be a big man at chapel, vice-president o' t' Cricket League, on t' hospital committee, an' so forth – eh?

ANNIE: Yes, Albert, you've done very well.

PARKER (*complacently*): I know I 'ave. An' mind you, it's not altered me much. I'm not like some of 'em. No swank about me – no la-di-dah – *I'm a plain man.*

ANNIE (*rather sadly*): Yes, Albert, you are.

PARKER (*looking at her suspiciously*): Well, what's wrong wi' it? You're not going to tell me that at your time o' life—

ANNIE (*indignantly cutting in*): My time of life!

PARKER: Well, you're no chicken, are yer? And I say, you're not going to tell me now, at your time o' life, you'd like a bit o' swank an' la-di-dah!

ANNIE (*wistfully*): I've sometimes wondered—

PARKER (*brushing this aside*): Nay, nay, nay, nobody knows better than me what you'd like. An' you know very well what a good husband I've been: steady—

ANNIE (*rather grimly*): Yes, you've been steady all right, Albert.

PARKER (*complacently*): That's what I say. Steady. Reliable. Not silly wi' my money—

ANNIE (*same tone*): No, Albert, your worst enemy couldn't
say you'd ever been silly with your money.

PARKER (*complacently*): And yet at the same time – not stingy.
No, not stingy. Everything of the best – if it could be
managed – everything of the best, within reason, y'know,
within reason.

ANNIE: Yes, within reason.

PARKER (*in a dreamy ecstasy of complacency*): Always reasonable
– and reliable. But all the time, getting on, goin' up i' the
world, never satisfied with what 'ud do for most men – no,
steadily moving on an' on, up an' up – cashier, manager,
share in the business – councillor this year, alderman next,
perhaps mayor soon – that's how it's been an' that's how
it will be. Y'know, Annie, I've sometimes thought that
right at first you didn't realize just what you'd picked out
o' t' lucky bag. Ay! (*Contemplates his own greatness, while she
watches him coolly.*)

ANNIE (*after a pause*): Well, Albert, what's all this leading up
to?

PARKER (*recalled to his argument*): Oh! – Well, yer see, Annie,
I was just saying that I thought I'd been a good husband to
you. An', mind yer, I don't say you've been a bad wife –
no, I don't—

ANNIE (*dryly*): Thank you, Albert.

PARKER (*with immense patronage*): So I thought I'd just set your
mind at rest. Now don't you worry about this wedding
business. If there's been a slip up – well, there's been a slip
up. But I'll see you're all right, Annie. I'll see it's fixed up
quietly, an' then we'll go an' get married again – properly.
(*He pats her on the shoulder.*) I know my duty as well as t' next
man – an' I'll see that you're properly married to me.

ANNIE: Thank you, Albert.

PARKER: That's all right, Annie, that's all right. I don't say
every man 'ud see it as I do – but – never mind – I know
what my duty is.

ANNIE: And what about me?

PARKER (*puzzled*): Well, I'm telling yer – you'll be all right.

ANNIE: How d'you know I will?

PARKER (*hastily*): Now don't be silly, Annie. If I say you'll be all right, you ought to know by this time yer *will* be all right.

ANNIE (*slowly*): But I don't think I want to be married to you.

PARKER (*staggered*): What!

ANNIE (*slowly*): You see, Albert, after twenty-five years of it, perhaps I've had enough.

PARKER (*horrified*): 'Ad enough!

ANNIE: Yes, had enough. You talk about your duty. Well, for twenty-five years I've done my duty. I've washed and cooked and cleaned and mended for you. I've pinched and scrimped and saved for you. I've listened for hours and hours to all your dreary talk. I've never had any thanks for it. I've hardly ever had any fun. But I thought I was your wife and I'd taken you for better or worse, and that I ought to put up with you—

PARKER (*staring, amazed*): Put up with me!

ANNIE (*coolly*): Yes, put up with you.

PARKER: But what's wrong with me?

ANNIE (*coolly*): Well, to begin with, you're very selfish. But then, I suppose most men are. You're idiotically conceited. But again, so are most men. But a lot of men at least are generous. And you're very stingy. And some men are amusing. But – except when you're being pompous and showing off – you're not at all amusing. You're just very dull and dreary—

PARKER: Never!

ANNIE (*firmly*): Yes, Albert. *Very* dull and *very*, *very* dreary and stingy.

PARKER (*staring at her as if seeing a strange woman*): 'As somebody put you up to this?

ANNIE: No, I've thought it for a long time.

PARKER: How long?

ANNIE: Nearly twenty-five years.

PARKER (*half dazed, half indignant*): Why – you – you – you little *serpent*!

ANNIE (*ignoring this*): So now I feel it's time I enjoyed myself a bit. I'd like to have *some* fun before I'm an old woman.

PARKER (*horrified*): Fun! Fun! What do you mean – fun?

ANNIE (*coolly*): Oh – nothing very shocking and terrible – just getting away from you, for instance—

PARKER (*in loud pained tone*): Stop it! Just stop it now! I think – Annie Parker – you ought to be ashamed of yourself.

ANNIE (*dreamily*): Well, I'm not. Bit of travel – and liveliness – and people that are amusing – and no wool business and town councillors and chapel deacons—

PARKER (*shouting angrily*): Why don't you dye your hair and paint your face and go on t' stage and wear tights—?

ANNIE (*wistfully*): I wish I could.

As PARKER groans in despair at this, RUBY looks in.

RUBY (*loudly and cheerfully*): Mr Soppitt says if you haven't finished yet yer better 'urry up or go somewhere else to 'ave it out 'cos they're all coming in 'ere.

PARKER (*angrily*): Well, we 'aven't finished.

ANNIE (*coolly*): Yes, we have.

RUBY nods and leaves the door open.

PARKER (*loudly*): Now listen, Annie, let's talk a bit o' sense for a minute—

ANNIE: They'll all hear you – the door's open.

PARKER: Nay – damn it—!

Goes to shut door, but SOPPITT and CLARA enter.

SOPPITT (*amused*): Hello, Albert – what's made you look so flabbergasted?

PARKER (*annoyed*): If I want to look flabbergasted, then I'll look flabbergasted, without asking your advice, Herbert.

SOPPITT: Hanky-panky!

G

PARKER: Now shut up! 'Ere, Clara, yer wouldn't say I was stingy, would yer?

CLARA: Well, you've never been famous for getting your hand down, have you, Albert?

PARKER (*indignantly*): I've got my 'and down as well as t' next man. I've always paid my whack, let me tell yer. Call a chap stingy just because he doesn't make a big show – 'cos he isn't – er—

ANNIE (*burlesqueing his accent, coolly*): La-di-dah!

SOPPITT: Now stop tormenting him, Annie.

PARKER (*indignantly*): Tormenting me! Nobody'll torment me. And I like that coming from *you*, Herbert, when you've been a byword for years.

CLARA (*angrily*): A byword for what?

PARKER: For years.

CLARA: Yes, but a byword for years for what?

PARKER: Oh! Henpecked! Ask anybody who wears trousers in your house!

ANNIE: Albert, don't be so vulgar!

PARKER: Why, a minute since you wanted to wear tights.

ANNIE: Only in a manner of speaking.

PARKER: How can it be in a manner of speaking? – 'cos either you're wearing tights or you're not.

Enter LOTTIE *and* JOE HELLIWELL.

LOTTIE: What's this about tights?

PARKER: Now you'll clear out right sharp – if you'll take my tip.

LOTTIE: And I'll bet it's the only kind of tip you do give, too. (*To Annie.*) He looks stingy to me!

PARKER: Stingy! If anyone says that again to me tonight – I'll – I'll give 'em jip.

Exit PARKER.

HELLIWELL: For two pins I'd either leave this house myself or else clear everybody else out. I've never seen such a place – there's folk nattering in every damn corner!

ANNIE: Where's poor Maria?

SOPPITT: Clara!

Exeunt SOPPITT, CLARA *and* ANNIE.

HELLIWELL: Now, Lottie, be reasonable. A bit o' devil-
ment's all right, but I know you don't want to make real
mischief—

LOTTIE: Where's the mischief come in? Didn't you say –
more than once – that if you hadn't been married already—?

HELLIWELL (*urgently to her*): Now, you know very well that
were only a bit o' fun. When a chap's on a 'oliday in a place
like Blackpool an' gets a few drinks inside 'im, you know
very well he says a lot o' damn silly things he doesn't
mean—

LOTTIE (*indignantly*): Oh – I see. Just tellin' me the tale an'
then laughing at me behind my back, eh?

HELLIWELL (*urgently*): No, I don't mean that, Lottie. Nobody
admires you more than I do. You're a fine lass and a good
sport. But you've got to be reasonable. Coming 'ere *like
this*, when you know as well as I do, it were just a bit o'
fun!

MARIA *enters. She is dressed to go out, and is carrying some
housekeeping books, some keys, and several pairs of socks.*

MARIA (*at door, leaving it open; grimly*): Just a minute, Joe
Helliwell!

HELLIWELL (*groaning*): Oh – Christmas! (*Then sees she has
outdoor things on.*) 'Ere, Maria, where are yer going?

MARIA (*determined, but rather tearful*): I'm going back to me
mother's.

HELLIWELL: *Your mother's!* Why, if you go to your mother in
this state o' mind at this time o' night, you'll give her a
stroke.

LOTTIE: That's right. She must be about ninety.

MARIA (*angrily*): She's seventy-two. (*Pauses.*) And mind your
own *business*. I've got some of it 'ere *for you*.

LOTTIE: What do you mean?

MARIA (*indicating things she's carrying*): Some of your new business, an' see 'ow you like it. You'll find it a change from carrying on wi' men behind the bar.

HELLIWELL: What in the name o' thunder are you talking about?

MARIA: I'm talking about 'er. If she wants my job, she can 'ave it.

LOTTIE: ⎫ 'Ere, just a minute—
HELLIWELL: ⎭ Now listen, Maria—

MARIA (*silencing them by holding up keys and rattling*): There's all t' keys, an' you'd better start knowing where they fit. (*Puts them on table behind settee.*) An' don't forget charwoman's just been sacked, an' I don't expect Ruby'll stay. You'll have to manage by yourself a bit. An' greengrocer calls at ten and the butcher calls at half-past—

HELLIWELL (*shouting*): What does it matter when t'butcher calls?

MARIA (*calmly*): I'm talking to 'er, not to you. (*To Lottie, who looks astonished.*) These is the housekeeping books an' you'll 'ave to 'ave 'em straight by Friday or he'll make a rumpus. 'Ere you are.

LOTTIE (*backing away*): I don't want 'em.

HELLIWELL (*harassed*): 'Course she doesn't—

MARIA: She can't run this house without 'em. You said so yourself. (*Throws books on to settee.*)

HELLIWELL: I know I did, but it's nowt to do with 'er.

MARIA: Then what did she come 'ere for? (*To Lottie, producing socks.*) An' look, 'ere's five pairs of his socks and one pair of woollens (*hangs them on back of settee*) that wants darning, and you'd better get *started* on 'em. An' upstairs you'll find three shirts and two more pairs of woollens you'll 'ave to do tomorrow, an' you'd better be thinking o' tomorrow's dinner, 'cos he always wants something *hot* an' he's very particular— (*Turns towards door.*)

LOTTIE (*aghast*): 'Ere, what do you think I am?

HELLIWELL: Now, Maria, you're getting it all wrong.

Nobody knows better than me what a good wife you've been. Now 'ave a bit of sense, love. It's all a mistake.

MARIA: And there's a lot of other things you'll have to manage, but while you're trying to manage them and him, too, I'll be at Blackpool.

She goes, followed by HELLIWELL.

Enter ORMONROYD.

ORMONROYD: I know that face.

LOTTIE: Harry Ormonroyd.

ORMONROYD: Lottie, my beautiful Lottie. And you haven't forgotten me?

LOTTIE: Forgotten you! My word, if you're not off I'll saw your leg off. 'Ere, you weren't going to take their photos?

ORMONROYD: Yes, group for *Yorkshire Argus*. Make a nice picture – very nice picture.

LOTTIE: Nice picture! Don't you know? Haven't they told you? (*Roars with laughter.*)

ORMONROYD: Here now, stop it, stop it. Have a drink of port.

LOTTIE: Well, I suppose I might.

ORMONROYD: Certainly, certainly. Liberty 'All here tonight.

LOTTIE: Oh – it's Liberty Hall right enough. Chin – chin.

ORMONROYD: All the best, Lottie.

LOTTIE: Nice drop of port wine this. Joe Helliwell does himself very well here, doesn't he?

ORMONROYD: Oh, yes, Lottie, you'll find everything very comfortable here. 'Ere, somebody told me you were back at the Talbot.

LOTTIE: I was up to Christmas. Who told you? Anybody I know?

ORMONROYD (*solemnly*): Yes – now just a minute. You know him. I know him. We both know him. I have him here on the tip of my tongue. Er— (*but can't remember*) no. But I'll get him, Lottie, I'll get him.

LOTTIE: Then I had to go home. Our Violet – you remember

our Violet – she married a sergeant in the Duke of Welling-ton's – the dirty Thirty-Thirds – and now she's in India.

ORMONROYD (*remembering, triumphantly*): Tommy Toothill!

LOTTIE: What about him?

ORMONROYD (*puzzled by this*): Nay, weren't you asking about 'im?

LOTTIE: No, I've something better to do than to ask about Tommy Toothill.

ORMONROYD (*still bewildered*): Quite so, Lottie. But what were we talking about him for? Didn't you say he'd gone to India?

LOTTIE: No, you fathead, that's our Violet. Oh – I remember, it must have been Tommy Toothill 'at told you I was working at the Talbot – d'you see?

ORMONROYD (*still bewildered*): Yes, I know it was. But what of it, Lottie? Aren't you a bit argumentative tonight, love?

LOTTIE (*good-naturedly*): No, I'm not, but you've had a couple too many.

ORMONROYD: Nay, I'm all right, love. 'Ere, what's happened to your Violet?

LOTTIE (*impatiently*): She married a sergeant and went to India.

ORMONROYD (*triumphantly*): Of course she did. Somebody told me – just lately.

LOTTIE: I told you.

ORMONROYD (*reproachfully*): Yes, I know – I can 'ear. But so did somebody else. I know – Tommy Toothill!

LOTTIE: You've got him on the brain. Then at Whitsun – I took a job at Bridlington – but I only stuck it three weeks. No life at all – I told 'em, I says: 'I don't mind work, but I do like a bit of life.'

ORMONROYD: I'm just the same. Let's 'ave a bit of life, I say. An' 'ere we are, getting down in dumps, just because Tommy Toothill's gone to India.

LOTTIE: He hasn't, you piecan, that's our Violet. Nay, Harry, you're giving me the hump.

ORMONROYD: Well, play us a tune, just for old times' sake.

LOTTIE: Aaaa, you silly old devil, I'm right glad to see you.

ORMONROYD: Good old times, Lottie, good old times.

    They sing. Interrupted by entrance of HELLIWELL, PARKER *and* SOPPITT.

HELLIWELL: Now what the hangment do you think this is – a taproom? *Yorkshire Argus* wants you on telephone.

LOTTIE: Come on, love, I'll help you.

HELLIWELL: And then get off home.

ORMONROYD: See you later.

    ORMONROYD *and* LOTTIE *exit.*

PARKER: Now, what's wanted now is a few serious words in private together.

HELLIWELL: Yes, yes, Albert. I know. But give a chap time to have a breather. I've just had to persuade Maria not to go back to her mother's.

PARKER: Why, what can her mother do?

HELLIWELL: Oh – don't start asking questions – just leave it, Albert, leave it, and let me have a breather.

    Enter the three wives, all with hats and coats on.

ANNIE: Now then – Albert – Joe – Herbert—

HELLIWELL: What is this – an ultimatum?

MARIA: Joe Helliwell, I want you to answer one question.

HELLIWELL: Yes, Maria?

MARIA: Joe, do you love me?

HELLIWELL (*embarrassed*): Now what sort of a question is that to come and ask a chap – here? Why didn't you ask me upstairs?

MARIA (*solemnly*): Once and for all – do you or don't you?

HELLIWELL: Yes, of course I do, love.

MARIA: Then why didn't you say so before?

    All three women sit down, take off hats.

PARKER (*as if beginning long speech*): And now we're all by ourselves it's about time we started to put our thinking caps on, 'cos we're not going to do any good running round the 'ouse argy-bargying—

MARIA: That's right, Albert.

PARKER: Yes, but let me finish, Maria. We—

He is interrupted by RUBY *appearing round door.*

RUBY (*loudly, cheerfully*): She's back!

MARIA: Who is?

RUBY: That Mrs Northrop. (*Withdraws, leaving door open.*)

HELLIWELL (*loudly, in despair*): Oh – Jerusalem – we don't want 'er 'ere.

MRS NORTHROP (*appearing, still carrying bag, and flushed*): If you don't want me here why did you send 'im round chasing me and askin' me to come back? Yer don't know yer own minds two minutes together. (*To Maria.*) You 'aven't settled up wi' me yet, y'know.

HELLIWELL (*annoyed*): Outside!

PARKER (*hastily, anxiously*): Half a minute, Joe, we can't 'ave her telling all she knows – we'll be t'laughing stock of Cleckleywyke tomorrow.

MRS NORTHROP (*contemptuously*): Yer've bin that for years, lad. I'd rather ha' Joe Helliwell nor you. Joe 'as 'ad a bit o' fun in his time, but you've allus been too stingy.

PARKER (*the word again*): Stingy! If anybody says that again to me tonight, they'll get what for, an' I don't care who it is.

HELLIWELL (*to Mrs Northrop*): I told you – outside – sharp!

MRS NORTHROP (*full of malice*): Suits me. I reckon naught o' this for a party. You can't frame to enjoy yourselves. But then there's one or two faces 'ere that'ud stop a clock, never mind a party. But wait till a few of 'em I know 'ears about it! You'll 'ear 'em laughing at back o' t'mill right up 'ere.

PARKER: Now we can't let her go i' that state o' mind.

CLARA: You ought to charge 'er with stealin'.

MRS NORTHROP (*horrified*): Stealin'! Why – for two pins – I'll knock yer lying 'ead off, missis. Never touched a thing i' my life that wasn't me own!

RUBY *looks in, and* MRS NORTHROP *sees her.*

What is it, love?

RUBY (*loudly, chiefly to* HELLIWELL): That photographer's asleep an' snoring be telephone.

HELLIWELL (*irritably*): Well, waken him up and' tell him to go home.

RUBY *withdraws.* MRS NORTHROP *takes charge again.*

MRS NORTHROP (*significantly*): An' I *could* keep me mouth shut if it were worth me while—

CLARA (*almost hissing*): That's blackmail!

SOPPITT (*hastily*): Shut up, Clara!

MRS NORTHROP (*looking at him*): Hello, *you've* come to life, 'ave yer?

HELLIWELL (*to Mrs Northrop*): How much d'you want?

MARIA (*angrily*): I wouldn't give her a penny.

CLARA (*quickly*): Nor me, neither.

PARKER (*quickly*): Can we trust 'er – we've no guarantee?

SOPPITT (*quickly*): She could sign something.

ANNIE (*quickly*): That'ud be silly.

MARIA (*quickly*): Not one single penny!

HELLIWELL (*angrily*): Will you just let *me* get a word in – an' be quiet a minute? Now then—

RUBY (*looking in*): Mr Helliwell!

HELLIWELL (*impatiently*): What?

RUBY: I wakened 'im an' told 'im to go 'ome. But 'e says 'e *is* at 'ome. (*Withdraws as* HELLIWELL *bangs and stamps in fury.*)

HELLIWELL (*at top of his voice*): What *is* this – a bloody mad-'ouse?

MERCER (*off, but approaching*): Mr Helliwell! Please!

HELLIWELL (*groaning*): Oh! – Jehoshaphat! – another of 'em!

MERCER *enters.*

MERCER (*sternly*): Mr Helliwell, I cannot allow you to use such language. It's quite unnecessary.

HELLIWELL (*protesting*): You wouldn't think so if—

MERCER (*cutting in*): Quite unnecessary. A little patience – a little quiet consideration – that's all that is needed.

HELLIWELL: What – with folk like her? (*Pointing to Mrs Northrop.*)

MERCER (*surprised and disapproving*): Mrs Northrop! What are *you* doing here?

MARIA (*quickly*): Making trouble!

MERCER (*before Mrs Northrop can speak*): Making trouble? (*He stoops a little, near her.*) And you've been drinking again.

MRS NORTHROP (*humble, crestfallen*): Only a drop or two – just because I was a bit upset—

MERCER (*accusingly*): And then you come and make a nuisance of yourself here. *T–t–t–t–t!* What's to be done with you? I am ashamed of you after all your promises.

MRS NORTHROP (*humble and flattering*): Oh – Mr Mercer – you're a wonderful man – an' you're t' only preacher i' Cleckleywyke worth listening to. (*To the others, roundly.*) Aaaa! – he's a fine preacher is Mr Mercer. Like – like a – gurt lion of a man! (*To Mercer admiringly.*) Ay, y'are that an' all.

MERCER (*briskly, masterfully*): Now, Mrs Northrop, flattery won't help. You've broken all your promises. I'm ashamed of you.

MRS NORTHROP (*almost tearful now*): Nay – Mr Mercer—

MERCER: Now – go home quietly—

MARIA (*quickly*): She'll tell all the town about us.

MERCER: We cannot allow that. Mrs Northrop, you must make me a solemn promise.

MRS NORTHROP (*looking up at him, humbly*): Yes, Mr Mercer.

MERCER: Now promise me, solemnly, you will tell nobody what you've heard here tonight. Now promise me.

MRS NORTHROP (*in solemn quavering tone*): I promise. (*Making suitable gestures.*) Wet or dry . . . may I die.

MERCER: T–t–t–t–t. But I suppose that will do. Now off you go, quietly home, and be a good woman. Good night, Mrs Northrop.

MRS NORTHROP (*humbly*): Good night, Mr Mercer, and thank you very much. (*Turns at door to address the company*.) Aaaa! – he's a gurt lion of a man— (*Fiercely, a parting shot.*) Worth all you lot put together.

She goes.

HELLIWELL (*with relief*): Well, we're rid o' one. (*To Mercer.*) Now have you studied that letter, Mr Mercer?

MERCER (*producing it*): I've considered it very carefully. (*Impressively.*) And you know what I think?

SEVERAL OF THEM (*eagerly*): No. Tell us. (*Etc.*)

MERCER (*slowly*): This letter – in my opinion – is perfectly genuine.

HELLIWELL (*disgustedly*): I thought you were going to tell us summat we didn't know.

MERCER (*ignoring this*): I am sorry to say it – but – quite obviously – you are, none of you, really married.

PARKER (*bitterly*): 'Ere don't rub it in. (*Hopefully.*) Unless, of course, you're prepared to marry us yourself – quietly – now.

MERCER (*indignantly*): Certainly not. Quite impossible.

HELLIWELL (*impatiently*): Well – what the hangment are we going to do, then?

MERCER (*turning to him impressively*): My dear sir— (*Then quickly.*) I don't know.

HELLIWELL (*disgusted*): Oh – Christmas!

MERCER: But if you want my final opinion, I think that if there were less bad temper and bad language in this house, and a little more patience and quiet consideration, you would have a better chance of settling your affairs.

HELLIWELL (*exasperated*): And *I* think I'm getting a bit tired o' you, Mr Mercer.

MERCER (*very angry, towering over Helliwell*): What! After wasting my time, you now have the audacity— Here!

HELLIWELL *flinches, but it is the letter he is being given.* Good night, sir. Good night, ladies.

He marches out and bangs doors. HELLIWELL *breathes heavily and wipes his face.*

HELLIWELL: Well, that's another we're rid of.

PARKER (*beginning in his usual style*): And now what's wanted—

CLARA (*cutting in, mimicking him*): Is a few serious words. We know. But what's really wanted now is a bit o' brainwork, and where we're going to get it from I don't know.

HELLIWELL (*severely to Clara*): You'll get it from me if you'll keep quiet a minute.

They concentrate hard, and now ORMONROYD, *still carrying a large glass of beer, comes in and sits down in the chair centre, while they stare at him in amazement and disgust.*

ORMONROYD (*cheerfully*): Now – let's see – what were we talking about?

PARKER (*angrily*): We weren't talking about anything to you.

ORMONROYD (*ignoring this*): I wouldn't object to a nice hand at cards. (*To Helliwell, who is looking exasperated.*) I like a game o' solo, don't you?

HELLIWELL: No. And I told you to get off 'ome.

ORMONROYD (*reproachfully*): Nay, but you want your photo o' t'group, don't you?

PARKER: You'll take no photos 'ere tonight.

ORMONROYD: Now it's a funny thing you should ha' said that. I'm a chap 'at notices things – I 'ave to be in my profession – an' I've been telling meself there's people 'ere in this 'ouse tonight who isn't easy in their minds. No, there's summat a bit off 'ere – just you see.

CLARA: Oh – for goodness' sake—

ORMONROYD (*to Helliwell*): And people has to be easy in their minds to be photographed. Nobody ever comes with the toothache, y'know, to 'ave their photos taken.

SOPPITT (*seriously*): No, I don't suppose they do. It never occurred to me – that.

ORMONROYD: Name, sir?

SOPPITT: Soppitt.

ORMONROYD: Ormonroyd 'ere. There's thought in this face. I'd like to do it some time in a nice sepia finish. Remind me, Mr Soppitt.

LOTTIE *enters.*

Ah, there y'are, Lottie. Join the company.

MARIA (*to Lottie*): I thought you'd gone long since.

HELLIWELL: You know very well you promised to go, half an hour since.

CLARA (*rises*): We ought to put police on you.

ORMONROYD: Now what's the idea of picking on Lottie? Why don't you live and let live? We're all in the same boat. We all come 'ere and we don't know why. We all go in our turn and we don't know where. If you are a bit better off, be thankful. An' if you don't get into trouble an' make a fool of yourself, well be thankful for that, 'cos you easily might. What I say is this – we're all human, aren't we?

ANNIE: Yes, and thank you, Mr Ormonroyd.

PARKER: What yer thanking him for? Who's he to start telling us what we ought to do?

CLARA: Impudence, I call it. (*Telephone rings.*)

ORMONROYD: Oh, me? I'm nothing much. But in case you want to be nasty, Councillor Albert Parker, just remember though I may be nothing I 'appen to work for a newspaper. Behind me stands the Press, don't forget that, an' the Press is a mighty power in the land today—

RUBY *enters.*

RUBY: Telephone went and when I says: 'Who is it?' chap said: '*Yorkshire Argus* – is Ormonroyd, our photographer there?' an' when I says: 'Yes, he's still 'ere,' he says: 'Well, tell him he's sacked.' You're sacked. I'm sorry.

RUBY *exits.*

ORMONROYD (*suddenly crushed*): So am I, lass. I left a bag in 'ere somewhere.

LOTTIE: You must have left it down at Lion, lad.

PARKER: I thought 'e couldn't carry corn.

ANNIE: Shut up, Albert.

LOTTIE: Nay, Harry, you silly old devil, it's not so bad.

ORMONROYD: It's not so good. Hard to know where to turn.

LOTTIE: Come on, lad, never say die. We've seen a bit of life an' we'll see some more before they throw us on the muck heap. (*To others.*) For two pins, I'd take him away now, and leave you to settle your own troubles – if you can.

HELLIWELL: Why – what's he got to do with our troubles?

LOTTIE: Plenty. Now, Harry, tell 'em where you were married.

ORMONROYD: Nay, Lottie, they don't want to hear about my bad luck.

PARKER: We've enough of our own, without his.

ANNIE: No, Albert. Come on, Mr Ormonroyd.

LOTTIE: Tell 'em where you were married.

ORMONROYD: Lane End Chapel – five-an'-twenty years since.

HELLIWELL: 'Ere, he must be in t'same boat with us then.

ORMONROYD: Just another o' my bits of bad luck.

CLARA: We can understand that all right.

LOTTIE: Yes, but Harry 'ere had separated from his wife and they wanted to be free.

HELLIWELL: Well, what were they worrying for? They were free. Parson hadn't proper qualifications.

LOTTIE: Hold on a minute . . . go on, Harry.

ORMONROYD: I know he hadn't. Wife found that out. But what she'd forgotten, till I got a copy o' t'certificate, is that in them days – twenty-five years since – chapel wedding – registrar had to be there an' all – to sign certificate.

PARKER: Joe, he's right.

ORMONROYD: I know damn well I'm right. I've been carrying certificate for months trying to find a loophole in it – see for yourself.

CLARA: Are we married after all?

HELLIWELL: Yes, of course we are. If parson didn't tie us up, registrar did – all legal – as right as ninepence.

CLARA: Aaaaa, thank God!

MARIA: Mr Ormonroyd, this is best night's work you ever did. Thank you.

LOTTIE: Now then, Harry, buck up, lad. Why don't you take that little photo shop in Blackpool again?

ORMONROYD: Nay, it 'ud cost me about a hundred pound to start it again – and I haven't a hundred shillings – an' I know you haven't.

LOTTIE: No, but there's folk here who'd never miss it.

PARKER: 'Ere, steady.

ANNIE: Albert, stingy again?

PARKER: Nay, never – if that's how you feel—

HELLIWELL: We'll soon fix you up, Ormonroyd lad, leave it to me. By gow, you've taken a load off my mind— Aaaaa— Now then, everybody, let's brighten up. (*At door.*) Who'll give us a song? Ruby . . . Ruby . . . bring some more drinks, lass. Owt you've got.

ANNIE: Let's sing a bit.

ORMONROYD: Lottie's the one. Come on, Lottie, play us a tune.

CLARA: Now then, Herbert Soppitt, you see, I am your wife after all.

SOPPITT: Yes, Clara, and I hope we'll be very happy. But we won't be if you don't drop that tone of voice. I don't like it.

CLARA: Yes, Herbert.

SOPPITT *begins to sing.*

PARKER: 'Ere, Joe, you wouldn't say I was dull and dreary, would you?

HELLIWELL: Ay, a bit, Albert.

PARKER: Well, that beats me. I've always seemed to myself an exciting sort of chap. (*To Annie.*) Anyhow, stingy or whatever I am, I'm still your husband.

ANNIE: So it looks as if I'll have to make the best of you.

MARIA: We'll all have to make the best of each other. But then, perhaps it's what we're here for.

HELLIWELL: That's right, love.

PARKER: Well, we'd better see if we can have some of this fun of yours you talk about.

ANNIE: Aaaa, it doesn't matter, Albert.

PARKER: It does. I say we'll have some fun. (*Takes her hand and begins singing. They are all singing now.*)

ORMONROYD (*loudly*): All in your places. We'll have this group yet, and to hell with the *Yorkshire Argus*! Now, steady – steady – everybody.

Enter RUBY. *The flashlight goes off and* RUBY *drops her tray. But they are all singing as curtain falls.*

END OF PLAY

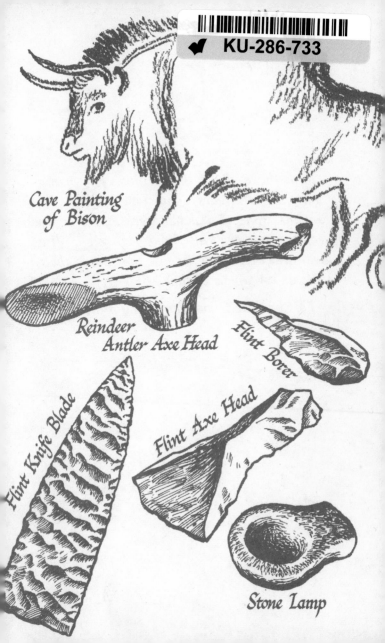

Cave Painting
of Bison

Reindeer
Antler Axe Head

Flint Borer

Flint Knife Blade

Flint Axe Head

Stone Lamp

Series 561

Men have lived in Britain for many thousands of years, and long before the Romans came the islands were inhabited by people whom we call Stone Age men. We give them this name because they made their tools and weapons of flint.

This book tells you something of how they lived.

Stone Age Man in Britain

by L. DU GARDE PEACH, M.A., Ph.D., D.Litt.

with illustrations
by JOHN KENNEY

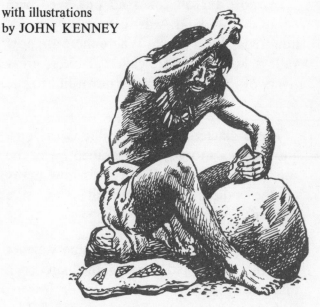

Publishers : Ladybird Books Ltd . Loughborough
© Ladybird Books Ltd (formerly Wills & Hepworth Ltd) 1961
Printed in England

STONE AGE MAN IN BRITAIN

The British Isles were not always the green and pleasant land in which we live to-day. Many thousands of years ago they were not even islands. The Straits of Dover did not exist, and England was joined to France by dry land.

In those far off times no one lived here because the land was covered with ice hundreds of feet thick. Where there are now valleys, were what are called glaciers: great rivers of ice slowly moving down hill to the sea.

These glaciers weighed millions of tons, and as they moved, they scraped away the rocky sides of the hills. This is how many of the valleys in the British Isles were formed.

Then slowly the climate became warmer and the ice melted, leaving the bare rock underneath. There were no trees or flowers, and many hundreds of years passed before the land was fit for men to live in.

4

7214 0169 4

Even before the trees and grass began to grow in Britain, the earliest men ever to live here came across the dry land from France.

These men and women were very different from the men and women of to-day. If we could see them, we should probably think that they were not human beings at all, because they were covered with hair and had fierce animal-like faces.

We should be wrong. These men of thousands of years ago were able to talk and think, though only in a very simple way. They knew how to make some sort of clothes for themselves out of the skins of animals, and they lived together in little family groups.

They had not yet learned how to build even the simplest houses, and in winter they must have been very uncomfortable, as well as being constantly in danger from wild beasts.

Near Torquay, in Devon, there is a cave called Kent's Cavern. This is one of the caves in which these men lived, more than ten thousand years ago.

There are many of these caves in England and in countries on the Continent. We know that these people lived in them, because buried in the clay or soil of the floors we find the charred bones of the animals which they hunted for food.

On the rocky walls of some of these caves in France, there are drawings of horses and deer and other animals. These are amazingly well done, and show the sort of animals which were living at that time.

Writing had not been invented in those days, but from these pictures and such stone tools as have been found in the caves, we can get some idea of the way these people lived, long before the dawn of history.

These men and women are our ancestors, and it is interesting to all of us to know something about their daily lives.

Perhaps the most important thing about them is that they knew how to make fire, probably by rubbing very dry sticks together. This made a great difference to their lives, because it meant that they could cook their food.

They had, of course, no iron or steel knives, or anything at all made of metal. Their spears and cutting tools were made of flint, which they chipped to a sharp edge and used for all purposes.

Nor had they any pottery, because they had not found out how to model clay and harden it in a fire.

We must think of these animal-like people as having none of the things which we use every day of our lives.

There are no dangerous wild animals in Britain to-day, but when these people lived here they had very often to hide from the many savage beasts which roamed the country.

Amongst these were huge animals which no longer exist anywhere on the earth, such as the mammoth. This was an animal larger than an elephant, and which was very dangerous.

Other wild and dangerous animals were savage sabre-toothed tigers and cave bears, as well as the woolly rhinoceros—animals which have now entirely disappeared.

These animals were hunted with flint weapons and with a thing called a bolas. This was a long cord made of skin or sinews, with a stone at each end. When it was thrown at an animal, it wrapped round the animal's legs so that it fell down. It could then be killed with a flint spear.

About six or seven thousand years ago, some new people came across the dry land into England. We call them the Neolithic people, and we know that they were much more intelligent than the men who lived in caves.

These new people were still dressed in the skins of animals, but they had found out how to make bows and arrows. This meant that they could hunt the wild animals with far less danger to themselves, because they could shoot them from a distance with their arrows.

One of the main reasons why men are different from animals is that men have brains which can think and remember. The cave man's brain was undeveloped, and he did not think very much. The Neolithic men had better brains, and when they saw things happening they wanted to know why they happened. This desire to find out why things happened was the beginning of all civilisation.

Let us look for a moment at the kind of country which these new people found when they crossed from France over the dry land, which in those days joined France and England.

There were, of course, no roads or houses, and no fields or hedges. Instead of these things, the newcomers found forests and swamps in the valleys, and chalk uplands or heather-covered hills.

If you look at what is called a contour map of the British Isles, you will see where the hills are situated. It was on these that Neolithic men and women mostly lived.

There was a good reason for this. They had no steel axes with which to cut down the trees of the forests, and even if they had been able to do so, they could not have drained the swampy land on which the forests grew. To live on the dry chalk hills, like the South Downs, was much easier for them, and it is here that we find the remains which tell us all we know about them.

We do not know what language these people spoke, or what sort of names they had for one another. If a man could run very fast they probably called him Quick Foot, of course in their own language. Let us see how he lived.

Quick Foot was not satisfied to live in a cave, like the people who came when the ice disappeared. He wanted to live on the dry, chalky soil of the South Downs, so he had to think about making a house or hut for himself and his family.

First he dug a hole in the ground, about two feet deep, and piled stones and turf round the edge until there was a wall four or five feet high. Across the top he put branches of trees and covered them with grass and reeds, with a layer of turf or skins on top.

It was not a very comfortable house, but Quick Foot was very proud of it. It kept out the rain and the snow, and it was certainly warmer than a cave.

Now that Quick Foot had a hut, he could think about making flint knives and arrow-heads, with which to go hunting.

In order to do this, he looked about for a large piece of flint, a shiny sort of stone which splits up into sharp flakes. When he found one, he hammered it with another stone until he had got a lot of sharp-edged pieces.

He next looked the pieces over very carefully. Some of them were no use at all, but some were long and thin, and very nearly the right shape for knives or arrow-heads.

Quick Foot had plenty of time and a lot of patience, and all day long he sat carefully chipping at the little flakes of flint and rubbing them on hard rocks, until they were beautifully shaped arrow-heads, or thin sharp knives with which to skin the animals he killed.

Besides hunting animals for food, these Neolithic men used their skins to make clothes for themselves and their wives and children.

The people who had lived in caves used the skins just as they were, but this was not good enough for the men who came after them. They cut the skins to the right shape with flint knives, and fastened the pieces together to make better fitting clothes.

It took these people a long time to think out how to make what we call a needle and thread. Even then it was only a thin piece of bone with a hole through one end, and some lengths of sinew.

Now they could sew the pieces of skin together and make quite warm, fur-lined clothes. What was more, they were very practical clothes: they kept out the rain and did not wear out.

The rivers of England were full of fish in those days, as they still are to-day, and sometimes men like Quick Foot would lie on the river bank and try to catch them in their hands.

This is very difficult, because fish are too slippery to hold, and they move very quickly. So these early fishermen tried hard to think of a better way of catching them.

Perhaps one day one of them was sewing some skins together, but at the back of his mind he was still trying to think of a good way to catch fish.

It could have been the bone needle which gave him the idea. "If I made a bone needle with a little hook on the end," he may have thought, "and then got a fish to swallow it, I could pull it out of the river."

So he scraped away at a little bone with his flint knife, and soon he had a fish-hook with which to go fishing in the rivers.

These men of long ago were now able to go hunting and fishing, and to sit around the fire in their huts when it was cold and wet outside.

But they wanted to travel further afield, and in a land of rivers and lakes they needed something in which to cross the water. So after a lot of thinking about it, they made a dug-out canoe.

Of course they had never seen one, but they had tried to sit on tree trunks floating in the water. These always rolled over, and they thought that if they could sit *in* the tree trunk, instead of *on* it, it would remain steady.

To hollow out a tree trunk with a flint knife was very difficult, but charred wood is much easier to scrape away. So they lit fires along the tree trunk and scraped away the charred wood as the fire burned down.

In this way they made canoes in which they could cross the lakes and rivers.

The people who had lived in caves had used tame dogs for hunting, but they had no other animals.

When the new people came across from France they brought with them some sheep, goats, pigs and small black cows. So instead of having to hunt for all their food, they had pigs for bacon and cattle for beef on the spot.

These people were farmers—very simple farmers—but the first of the millions of farmers who have lived on the soil of England ever since.

Up to this time no man had ever tasted anything like bread. Everybody had lived on meat of one sort or another, and the fruit and berries which they found growing wild.

The next step was to grow some sort of corn out of which to make bread.

We do not know how these people who lived here in Britain so long ago, first came to grow corn.

Perhaps Quick Foot's wife, or some other woman, threw away some grass seeds beside the hut and noticed that they grew. Then she may have planted some more, and when these grew, cooked them in milk from the cows or goats, and made a sort of porridge.

But the seeds became dry and hard, and perhaps she thought that if she rubbed them between two stones, they would make better porridge. To her surprise, they made something quite different.

By crushing the seeds she had made a rough sort of flour, and when it was cooked with water or milk, it became bread.

Everybody liked the new sort of food, so they planted more seeds, and made shallow holes in flat stones, with other stones fitting into them, to grind the seeds into flour.

People in Britain were now becoming more and more domesticated.

This means that instead of being wandering savages, they were living in villages of huts like the one Quick Foot had built, and working their little farms.

About this time another great advance was made towards better living conditions. The Stone Age men discovered how to make pottery.

Clay was abundant, and it was noticed that when it was shaped and exposed to the fire, it became hard and, what was more important, capable of keeping its shape and holding water.

Bowls and dishes made by these early people have been found. They were roughly shaped by hand and without the shiny glazed surface which our cups and saucers have to-day. But the most interesting thing about them is that the bowls all have a round or pointed base. This means that they were not intended to stand on a table. It is probable that they were propped up by stones, and that a fire was built round them to heat whatever they contained.

By this time men had discovered a new way of lighting a fire.

The cave men had rubbed dry sticks together, but this is a very slow and difficult way of making fire. One day one of the Neolithic men may have been chipping away at a flint to make a knife, and the sparks which always fly when flint is chipped may have fallen on some dry moss. Immediately the moss would have begun to smoulder, and when the man blew on it, it burst into flames.

Ever after that he and the other men carried pieces of flint and some dry moss about with them, so that they could easily light a fire whenever they wanted to.

It is interesting to remember that this way of making fire was still used until just over a hundred years ago, when matches were invented. Even to-day, a petrol lighter makes a spark in the same way, to set fire to the wick.

The huts built in the early days did not stand all alone on the South Downs. A lot of other men like Quick Foot had built huts just like his all around him. Probably a hundred families lived close together in a little village of huts, with a wall round it to keep out wild animals.

These little villages must always have had some man who was stronger or wiser than the others, and soon such a man might become the chief of a whole tribe living in different villages all over the Downs.

There were no roads or even footpaths in Britain when the cave men lived here, but now the people of one village often went to the other villages to exchange corn for fish or to bargain for flint tools.

On these journeys they always went by the easiest way, and soon beaten tracks were made through the woods or across the hills from one village to another.

These were the beginnings of the roads of Britain to-day.

There came a day when the men of another tribe thought that instead of raising their own cattle, it would be easier to steal the cows and sheep belonging to some nearby tribe.

So they came over the hills with their flint spears and their bows and arrows, and there was a fierce battle before they were beaten off.

Then all the men of the tribe got together and decided to make a strong fortress where they would be safe from attack.

They had no tools with which to build a stone castle, but they had bone shovels made from the shoulder blades of the deer which they hunted for food.

With these they dug a deep ditch, piling up the earth behind it, around the top of a hill. Many of these hill-top forts can still be seen in Britain.

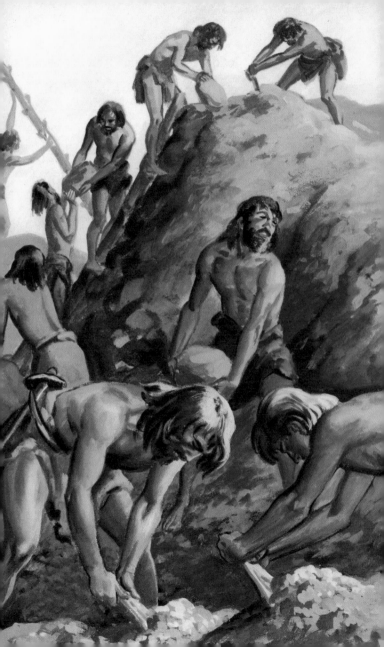

When a leader died, the whole tribe gathered together to make a tomb worthy of their chief.

By piling together a number of heavy stones they built a sort of stone hut, roofed over with larger flat slabs of rock. Inside it, with the body of their chief, they left his flint weapons and ornaments.

Then over the stone hut they raised a great mound of earth. Many of these burial mounds still exist in Britain.

There were in those days no churches, because these people worshipped the sun. They realized that without it, life could not exist, so they built great circles and avenues of stone at places where, at certain times of the year, they came for their religious festivals.

Things did not change quickly in those days, and even a thousand years after Quick Foot died, the people were still living in the same kind of huts, using the same sort of flint knives, and sewing the skins of animals together for clothes.

But they had learned how to shape great blocks of stone by hammering them with other stones, and the bowls which they made were decorated with patterns cut in the wet clay before they were hardened in the fire.

About two-thousand years before the birth of Christ, there must have been some wise and powerful man who was the chief of a great many tribes and villages in the south of England.

He and the chief men of all the tribes decided to build a great temple for the sun god.

The temple which they built still stands on Salisbury Plain in Wiltshire. It is called Stonehenge.

The work of building Stonehenge must have employed many hundreds of men, because the great stones were brought from many miles away. Some of them came from quarries in Wales, a distance of 150 miles from where they now stand.

Even to-day, with cranes and ships and railways, it would be quite a difficult task to bring these great stones, some of which weighed nearly thirty tons, from Pembroke-shire to Salisbury Plain.

We know the quarries from which the stones came, but we can only guess how these people quarried them, nearly four-thousand years ago.

Probably they drove wooden pegs into cracks in the cliffs and then poured water on them. As the wet wood expanded, it split great pieces of stone away from the cliffs' sides.

The stones had now to be shaped. This was done by hammering them with other stones. Hundreds of men must have been busy for many months, slowly flattening out the rough surfaces and shaping the corners.

The leading men of the tribes were very busy all this time arranging how the stones were to be brought across rough country to Wiltshire.

They may have come by way of where Gloucester stands to-day. Strong tree trunks would be used as levers to lift one end at a time, whilst other tree trunks were placed under them as rollers. Then hundreds of men would haul the stones along, a few yards at a time, pulling on ropes made of plaited leather.

Or they may have been levered on to large rafts and floated along the Bristol Channel, and up the River Avon to some-where near Bath.

All this must have taken years, but at last they were ready for setting up.

These early builders now had to think out some way of making the stones stand upright.

Quite recently some of these stones which had fallen down, have been lifted upright by powerful cranes. Even so, it was very difficult and took a long time.

The man who ordered the building of Stonehenge had no cranes. But he had thousands of men to work for him, so he made them start by digging a hole for each stone to stand in. Then the men piled up a sloping mound of earth with a straight up and down end at the edge of the hole.

The stone was next hauled up the slope on rollers until it overbalanced and one end fell into the hole. The mound of earth was then removed and the hole filled up round the stone.

Many of the stones still stand where they were first set up. They have not moved an inch in four-thousand years.

So, you see, although they could not write their story in words for us to read, we know quite a lot about these men who lived in Britain so long ago.

How do we know all this?

It is by the patient work of men and women who dig in the ground in places where Neolithic men lived, and who find the flint tools which they used and the simple articles of bone and pottery which they made.

To-day we should call these early inhabitants of Britain savages. But although the Stone Age men were a very primitive race, every now and then there would be amongst them some man like Quick Foot who could think better than the others. Then some small advance would be made— like the discovery of pottery or the use of the roller and lever.

They were not savages. They were the dim beginnings of the modern civilisation in which you and all of us now live.

Arrow Heads

Spearhead

Hand Axe

Bone Needles

Cooking Pot

Cutting Tool

Cave Painting of Horse

Bone Harpoon